PATIENTS

BRITT BERRETT

COME

PAUL SPIEGELMAN

SECOND

LEADING CHANGE *by*
CHANGING *the* WAY
YOU LEAD

AN **INC.** ORIGINAL

An Inc. Original
New York, NY
www.inc.com

Distributed by Greenleaf Book Group LLC

For ordering information or special discounts for bulk purchases, please contact Greenleaf Book Group LLC at PO Box 91869, Austin, TX 78709, 512.891.6100.

Design and composition by Greenleaf Book Group LLC
Cover design by Greenleaf Book Group LLC

Publisher's Cataloging-In-Publication Data

(Prepared by The Donohue Group, Inc.)

Berrett, Britt.

  Patients come second : leading change by changing the way you lead / Britt Berrett, Paul Spiegelman. -- 1st ed.

    p. ; cm.

  Issued also as an ebook.

  ISBN: 978-0-9888428-0-9 (hardbound)

  1. Health facilities--Personnel management. 2. Health facilities--Employees. 3. Medical personnel--Attitudes. 4. Leadership. I. Spiegelman, Paul. II. Title.

RA971.35 .B47 2013

362.110683   2013900576

Part of the Tree Neutral® program, which offsets the number of trees consumed in the production and printing of this book by taking proactive steps, such as planting trees in direct proportion to the number of trees used: www.treeneutral.com

Printed in the United States of America on acid-free paper

TreeNeutral

16 17 18 19 20 21   12 11 10 9 8 7 6

First Edition

This book is dedicated to the patients and their families who we are so fortunate to serve each day.

CONTENTS

What's Up with the Title?

Be honest: Why did you pick up this book? Was it because of the title? If so, that's okay—we hoped it might work out that way. "But what does the title mean?" you might now be asking. As a way to answer that question, kick-start the discussion, and expose the true intent of this book, we'd like to share a recent e-mail dialogue we engaged in (with someone who we hope will be reading this book):

Hi, Paul.

I just returned from The Beryl Institute Conference (which was great!), where I heard you discussing your upcoming book, *Patients Come Second*. I think you should know that among conference attendees, there was a lot of negative discussion about the title. There we were, four hundred patient experience leaders, most of whom have been championing the patient experience for years. And now a respected, prestigious, distinguished leader—you—says, "Patients come second."

I am writing because I strongly encourage you to change the title of your book. Is your title catchy? Yes! But you are an influential leader, and to say that patients are behind employees in terms of priority is to give health care leaders more excuses for not holding employees accountable for their behavior toward patients. This also gives employees more reason to say, "I'm not being cared for well enough in my job, so I can't (or won't) be caring with patients."

I believe that your book title is very destructive and invites reviews and blog posts that will be unnecessarily negative. Will publicity, whether negative or positive, sell books? Perhaps . . . but I see you as a mission-driven person who—beyond making money—wants to do good in the world. I certainly know that we must create a healthy culture and caring environment for our employees if we expect them to care well for patients, but there is no need to rank the two in order of who is more important, patients or employees. In your book, surely you can make all your points about the importance of the employee experience without using this damaging title.

Thank you for your consideration.

Warm regards,
Wendy L.

This is how we responded:

Hi, Wendy.

Thanks so much for taking the time to write to me. I'm glad you enjoyed the conference and sorry we didn't get the opportunity to say hello in person. I also appreciate the feedback on the book's title and will share your comments with Britt (my coauthor). I'll genuinely take the suggestion under consideration, but first let me respond here to a few of your concerns.

As you surmised, this project has nothing to do with selling books or making money. I write books to try to deliver a message that can change the way business is done, both inside and outside of health care. While the title may seem controversial, once you read the book (and I hope you will), you'll see that we are all after the same thing: improving the experience for the patient. There was once a popular business book called *The Customer Comes Second*. That title could have provoked the same response, but it revealed an important truth that spoke to people in the business world. Let's face it: Employees in most companies get treated as second-class citizens. If that's the case, how can we expect them to treat customers well? The same is true for employees in the health care field.

In health care, we need a model for the delivery of a great experience for each patient. It is not a question of ranking what is more important, but a question of leading and lagging indicators of success. In that regard, I firmly believe (and there is increasing data to back this up) that the most successful organizations with the most loyal customers (or patients) have focused first on an internal culture of engagement, where leadership shows a genuine interest in the growth and development of its people. If you do that, accountability will only increase, not create excuses for lack of execution.

When you read the book, you will learn about an ongoing debate between me and Dr. David Feinberg, CEO of UCLA Health System in Los Angeles. He believes that if each employee just focuses on the next patient, he or she will be a happy employee. Dr. Feinberg may be right, but I believe that the better we feel about ourselves, the better we treat others.

Our industry needs to be shaken up a bit. My hope is that our book (with whatever title we finally choose) will stir healthy conversation and action to improve internal cultures in health care. It is sorely needed.

Thanks again for reaching out—it sounds as though we've already stirred the pot. I appreciate all the work you are doing in the industry.

Best,

Paul

Since you're reading this now, you might have guessed that although we did consider Wendy's suggestion to change the book's title, ultimately we stuck with our gut instinct. Why? For the very reasons she was opposed to it: The title is controversial and edgy, and it borders on being offensive. And guess what? That is exactly what we as an industry need in order to bring about change: a big, collective slap in the face! Then we can begin to embrace the responsibility of focusing on the team so we can bless lives with good health. We need to speak openly and honestly about how to improve the patient's experience. And that starts with the team doing the work.

Let us reiterate: Our intent in tackling this project isn't to make a bunch of money. The intent is to instigate a passionate discussion that will shake up our industry. Does anyone really believe that we are talking about ignoring the patient? If so, the content on the pages that follow will dispel that notion.

Wendy does raise an interesting point about accountability. But to us, comments like "Sure, this is easy to say, but my boss will never support it," or "I would like to do all that stuff, but my HR department doesn't get it," or even something like "I work in civil service, and we can't do that," are really just poor excuses. If you find yourself saying you cannot give exceptional care to a patient because your team isn't functional, you need to go back to the drawing board. Change your existing team or get a different team. Reorient current resources or pull in new resources. Tweak an existing strategy or create a new strategy. Change a player, change a couple players . . . change the way you lead! How else can you expect to care for your patients the way you must?

In our experience, the majority of health care workers want nothing more than to improve the patient experience. That's why they got into this field in the first place. But it is not always easy for them to do their best work. Ron Swinfard, CEO of Lehigh Valley Health System in Allentown, Pennsylvania, told us in a passionate moment:

> I really don't give a damn what model the federal government or the state government inflicts on us for how they want us to deliver care. As long as we as providers care about our patients and one another, we'll be successful. People will beat down our doors to get here, because they'll feel it.

We wholeheartedly agree! Providers must care about patients and one another—only then will we see the essential changes our health care system requires. Now, perhaps this is the biased perspective from a couple of veterans of the health care industry, but it's our opinion nonetheless. And guess what? We've put the effort into writing this book precisely to stir some dialogue and unleash people's passion on both sides of the debate.

Now, if your curiosity has been stoked, or even if you just want to find reasons to write us and tell us how wrong we are, turn the page and read on. We look forward to the debate that will follow!

CHAPTER ONE

What Does Come First?

The United States has the finest health care delivery system in the world, bar none. But it doesn't always seem that way—especially when you're the patient.

Consider the following story: A middle-aged husband—let's call him "Paul"—gets talked (we won't say "guilt-tripped") into getting a vasectomy. Now, getting a vasectomy means that your doctor is going to get very personal with you in a very meaningful way. It should also go without saying that you don't want the doc to screw anything up. That's why Paul first asked around for references from his coworkers and friends as a way to make sure he got the very best urologist on the case. It turns out that several people steered him to the same doctor—a particular guy who operated out of the local hospital. "He's the best there is," everyone gushed, so Paul went ahead and scheduled an appointment.

When Paul showed up for his first visit with the doctor—let's call him "Dr. Gillespie"—he ended up sitting in the waiting room for almost two hours before someone even acknowledged that he was there. When Paul was finally called into an examination room, a physician's assistant explained what was going to happen. "It's very quick, snip-snip," he told Paul. "We'll get you on the calendar for surgery next month."

"But wait!" said Paul. "Don't I get to meet the doctor?"

"No, you don't need to meet him," answered the PA as he handed Paul a piece of paper with the date of his surgery printed on it. "He's done thousands of these things. You don't have to worry about anything."

On his way to the car, Paul looked at the piece of paper in his hand. Then he simply crumpled it up and tossed it in the nearest trash can. "If someone is going to cut me down there, he needs to look at me up here," he said to himself, pointing to his eyes.

A few months later, with his wife still asking (we won't say "nagging") about the vasectomy, Paul connected with an old friend of his—a guy who operates a different local hospital. Let's call him "Britt." Paul told Britt about this predicament, and Britt suggested he make an appointment to see another doctor named, for our purposes, "Dr. Spock." Paul somewhat hesitantly agreed to call up the doc for an appointment.

This time, before he could even get in the door, Paul was told he needed to watch three ten-minute videos on YouTube that explained the risks of the surgery as a way to prepare him for his first visit. On the day of the appointment, this Dr. Spock met Paul not in the examination room but in the consultation room. Paul was already starting to feel more comfortable.

"Did you have a chance to watch the videos?" asked Dr. Spock.

Paul nodded.

"And did you have any questions about them or about the surgery?" the doc continued. Only after Dr. Spock had answered Paul's questions did he actually examine Paul, which he did in an efficient five minutes.

From Paul's point of view, Dr. Spock had done all he could to earn his trust. This time, Paul carried the piece of paper with his appointment date all the way home to his refrigerator door.

The best part, though, was that after the surgery was successfully completed, Paul received a handwritten note in the mail from the nurse who had discharged him. She wanted to make sure that everything was okay with him post-surgery. In other words, Dr. Spock and his team treated Paul with respect from start to finish—something that he appreciated immensely, especially when compared to his earlier experience with Dr. Gillespie's office. Want to guess whom Paul told his friends and colleagues to go see when they needed a vasectomy?

REFOCUSING ON WHAT REALLY MATTERS

If you didn't connect the dots from the vasectomy story, Paul and Britt are real-life characters. In fact, they're the fellows who have written this book. And yes, while we did change some names, the story itself is true—and was told with a key point in mind. Namely, that attention to the so-called patient experience is often lacking in today's health care arena.

What does "patient experience" mean, anyway? A group of patient experience leaders across the country, whose research was sponsored by The Beryl Institute, coined the following definition of patient experience: "the sum of all interactions, shaped by an organization's culture, that influence patient perception across the continuum of care." Here is a less MBA-like explanation: The patient experience centers around the story you tell your spouse when you get home from your appointment. Nobody comes home after a surgery saying, "Man, that was the best suturing I've ever seen!" or, "Sweet, they took out the correct kidney!" Instead, we talk about the people who took care of us, the ones who coordinated the whole procedure—everyone from the receptionist to the nurses to the surgeon. And we don't just tell these stories around the dinner table. We share our experiences through conversations with friends and colleagues and via social media sites like Facebook and Twitter.

When we asked Andy Leeka, CEO of Good Samaritan Hospital in Los Angeles, about how he defines patient experience, he told us this:

> There are a lot of phrases, technical terms, and acronyms that are thrown out and bandied about in healthcare discussions. "Patient-centered care" is one of them, used to describe the involvement of patients and their families in the decision-making process as you explore options for treatment. But what does this mean to an admitting clerk, laboratory phlebotomist, or patient transporter? It is important for leaders to demystify language so that every member of the team understands the goal and can have the authority to achieve it. "Patient-centered care" can be

summed up as the way I want my parents to be treated in a hospital. Period.

People cede a certain level of personal control when they become a patient. Whether they don't have the complete understanding of a procedure that will be performed on them or their clothes are taken from them and replaced by a short smock that opens in the back—they give up something. At that point, patients are vulnerable and rely upon one thing: trust. Trust that you are competent, have their best interests at heart, are prepared and able to perform, and will tell them the truth. They are relying on you after having met you only briefly. They are nervous, anxious, and are not at your hospital for entertainment or fun. They go to Disneyland for fun. At a hospital, they may be there to be healed, give birth, have diagnostic testing, and ultimately restore their life to normal. We owe it to them to take the best we have to offer and deliver it in the most caring, compassionate, and gentle manner we know—just like we would deliver it to our parents.

Case in point: A friend of ours, Melody Trimble, CEO of Sparks Health System in Fort Smith, Arkansas, shared with us the following story told by her human resources director:

A few weeks ago I was talking to a patient in the hallway, and he was telling me about the great experience he'd just had on one of the hospital floors. In the same breath, he told me about a terrible experience he'd had in another unit. The story was so intertwined that I couldn't keep up with when the good and the bad experiences had actually happened. As I continued to talk to him, I learned that the bad experience had been two years ago; the good experience had just concluded that day. Yet the patient was relating both stories as if they had just occurred.

My thought on the encounter was this: The patient experience starts whenever the patient thinks it starts. That might be when a potential patient hears a news story about us or when he or she calls in for an appointment. But the patient experience never ends, because it's not linear. We tend to think of it as linear, because that perspective helps us keep track of our work. But patients don't see the patient experience as a separate thing. It's just part of the web that is their life. That has very positive and negative consequences for those of us in health care. Because we're part of the patient's web, we can really advance Sparks Health System if we get it right. If we get it wrong, though . . .

This is such a poignant story because, let's face it, most of us would rank going to the doctor somewhere between watching *The Lion King* with your kids for the thousandth time and visiting your mother-in-law (just kidding, ladies—we love seeing you!). But building a relationship with a patient means that every interaction health care providers have with that patient really matters.

Given how nervous and keyed up we as patients usually are when we interact with our health care providers, because that's when we are likely to be at our most vulnerable, the experience of having someone say hello or take an extra minute to make sure we're okay—let alone send off a thank-you note!—can often outshine any experience we have in receiving the actual physical care. Don't forget the paradox we're talking about here: This is a business in which no one wants to be the customer!

The truth is that the patient experience now extends beyond the clinical result, beyond the four walls of the doctor's office or the hospital, to include anything from pre-care assessments to post-care phone calls and checkups. But an industry-accepted estimate holds that the average person comes to the hospital only once every seventeen years and to the emergency room once every three years. That means we don't get many shots to get it right.

To deliver a great experience, then, health care leaders have to care about their impact from all angles—each and every way they interact with their patients. That's why the off-putting story about "Dr. Gillespie," an all-too-common scenario these days, could be a competitive disadvantage for a doctor, a hospital, or an entire system of health care workers, especially given the rapidly changing health care market. It used to be that patients had limited choices when it came to whom they could see about their health care. This allowed the industry to develop a "build it and they will come" approach. Now, choice is the name of the game. For example, there are some 2,300 post–acute care home health agencies, skilled nursing and rehabilitation facilities, and other specialty niche services in the Dallas–Fort Worth area alone. And patients are taking advantage of this wide selection of health care options, with an increasing number relying on high-deductible insurance plans that allow individuals the freedom to choose their health care providers.

The availability of many health care options is a big part of the reason Bob Kelly, president of New York–Presbyterian Hospital, told us this:

> As the demands of health care are sort of evolving, no one can keep up with any of them, and so people change for a lot of reasons—but in general, they change because they have to. I think right now everyone is feeling like they have to change—the way we learned, the way we did things, isn't working anymore. The current model goes like this: You get sick, you come into the hospital, you see the doctor, we take care of you, we tell you to follow up but we don't know whether you do or not, we send you out, you either stay well or get sick again and come back, and it starts all over again. I don't think people are feeling ultimately like this is a great system.

We agree that change typically happens only when it is forced upon us—often by circumstance but also, at times, by the federal government, which has emerged as the largest and most influential player amid this jungle of providers. The government now limits reimbursement to providers based on positive patient feedback (HCAHPS scores) and low readmission rates, so delivering an exceptional patient experience could be the difference between financial success and failure for health care providers in the coming years. And while it is a big enough challenge to focus on our own organization, the changing market will force us to work more collaboratively with our competitors!

Wayne Lerner, CEO of Holy Cross Hospital in Chicago, framed it for us in this way:

> The future will not be centered around the hospital experience. It will be the entire patient experience, which includes more than hospitals. Organizations that used to be competitive will now need to work together. Just add that to the list of challenges!

This fact has not gone unnoticed by other health care executives. If you had surveyed the nation's top health care executives three years ago about what issues kept them up at night, patient experience wouldn't have even made the list. Today, patient experience is a top-three kind of issue, ranking even higher than cost reduction. Yet three-quarters of health care organizations have yet to define what patient experience means to them, let alone set aside money to address it. The more progressive executives who have tried to tackle the challenge head-on, however, have gone about trying to solve it in a backward manner. They have plowed money into adding more beds or developing new technology such as electronic medical records, all while overlooking the obvious solution: investing in their employees.

Hospitals have missed the point that the best way to improve the patient experience is to build better engagement with their employees, who will then provide better service and health care to patients. To put it another way: Patients come second.

DELIVERING AN EXCEPTIONAL EXPERIENCE

We know, we know—right about now you're saying something like, "What do you mean, 'patients come second'? Why would you focus on your employees if you want to improve the experience of the patient? Sounds like you guys must have written yourselves an extra prescription or two." Well, while we admit to being somewhat wacky and fun loving, we're stiff-lipped serious when it comes to the notion that an organization's culture—specifically, how engaged its employees are in their work—is the primary driver for delivering an exceptional patient experience. Bob Kelly from New York–Presbyterian Hospital offered an apt analogy: "Focusing on employee engagement is akin to being on an airplane and putting your oxygen mask on first, before attending to your kids. How can our people help their patients when they, too, are suffering?"

While this may seem counterintuitive to you, consider how important this topic is in the general world of business, where well-known and wildly successful CEOs Tony Hsieh of Zappos and Howard Schultz of Starbucks have written best-selling books about how they empowered their employees to deliver great experiences to their customers. But we have more than just anecdotal proof to lean on. In the 2007 book *Firms of Endearment: How World-Class Companies Profit from Passion and Purpose*, authors David Wolfe, Rajendra Sisodia, and Jagdish Sheth tracked a series of companies known for having strong employee cultures— a list that included such familiar names as Whole Foods, Harley-Davidson, and Patagonia. The authors found that the companies on their list produced an impressive 1,025 percent return for their investors over a ten-year period. In comparison, the companies in Standard & Poor's 500 index produced a mere 122 percent return over the same period. Not too shabby, right?

Well, it gets better. You've probably heard about or maybe even read the book *Good to Great* by Jim Collins, which, more than a decade after its initial publication, continues to top business book bestseller lists. But do you know what happened when the *Firms of Endearment* authors calculated the return on investment for the *Good to Great* companies over the same ten years? They found that these companies produced a 316 percent ROI—a satisfying result, but one that is less than one-third of the return produced by companies known more for their level of employee engagement than for their "greatness." To put it another way, employee engagement pays off big-time—something executives all around the country are beginning to realize.

The connection isn't lost on Ron Swinfard, CEO of Lehigh Valley Health System, who told us he uses symbolic imagery to get the point across: a slide presentation that shows several links in a chain, starting with employee satisfaction and leading to patient satisfaction and finally to financial success. "I tell my employees that this isn't just a feel-good idea; it is also a business strategy," Ron said.

Let's consider an everyday example of how this works. Say that you love starting off your mornings with a venti half-caf soy latte. Given the proliferation of Starbucks across the country you may, depending on where you live, have access to two, three, or even more locations where you can buy your coffee every morning. And for the most part, each cup will taste about the same. The key difference in where you choose to buy your latte, then, could be the location where you most enjoy interacting with the baristas. It might be an extra smile, a sincere word of thanks, or just the sight of an employee who seems to take great pleasure in frothing milk that can help start your day off right. A frown, a mixed-up order, or even a lack of eye contact, on the other hand, might result in a grumpy start to your day—and for that Starbucks location, a lost customer.

Now do you get it? The type of customer experience you receive begins with the employee who served you. "Engaged employees are willing to go the extra mile—for themselves, their coworkers, and their customers," explained our friend Dane Peterson, CEO of Emory University Hospital Midtown in Atlanta. "They seek out problems and work to solve them." And their customers take notice.

It's our contention that customers are smart. They can tell whether the stranger pouring their cup o' joe in the morning is fully engaged in his or her work. Sure, the barista could fake it by simply following the training script. But customers know—especially when something goes wrong with their order. What happens then, Mr. Unengaged Employee? Does your script cover the fact that you left out the milk or ground the wrong coffee bean? Great employees, on the other hand, will find solutions with a smile on their face—saving the relationship and maybe even making it stronger along the way.

The same principle holds true in health care. Whether you are purchasing a cup of coffee or having your hip replaced, your decision comes down to three elements: cost, quality, and service. The cost of health care here in the United States takes a backseat, of course, due to our reliance on third-party payers—insurance companies. Nor is quality the issue. Not only do we possess the best brick-and-mortar infrastructure around, we also have the best scientists who help us eradicate the most malicious of diseases and the greatest group of health care providers, who have pursued a higher calling by entering the field. This means that as the health care system here begins to shift to a more consumer-focused model, patients will increasingly base their purchasing decisions on where and who provide the best service. Steve Moreau, CEO of St. Joseph's Hospital of Orange in Orange County, California, explained it to us like this:

> I don't think you're going to get the kinds of very high patient satisfaction scores unless you do focus on the employee role. It is clear, though—and I'm certainly aware, because I've been at organizations that have all private rooms and million-dollar views—that not everybody can do that. We've been able to be highly competitive in the patient experience despite the fact that we don't have all private rooms and we don't have a million-dollar view, because we focus on what patients really care about when they're here, when they're vulnerable. They're not looking out the window. What they care about is the way they feel, the way you make them feel, and that is a result of the interaction with every person they come in contact with.

Patients expect that they're going to get the best care all the time. What they want is to feel that someone cares *about* them. That's not something you can do without engaging your employees. So I think that employee engagement is absolutely fundamental if we're going to accomplish what we need to accomplish.

While you might not think about it in terms of nurses, orderlies, and physicians providing a service to the customer, that's exactly what the patient is thinking. And that means delivering a great end result is just not good enough. A great result should be expected, whether you're delivering a baby or performing an appendectomy. But along with that, you also need to deliver an exceptional experience. We are suggesting (no, we are insisting) that all three of these elements—cost, quality, and service—are the keys to your success in pleasing your patients.

But rather than tackle those elements individually, we've found a way to do all three at once. And we're going to show you how to build an organizational culture that delivers great patient experiences by tapping a resource you may have overlooked: your own employees. Tony Armada, CEO of Advocate Lutheran General Hospital in Chicago, put it like this:

> At the end of the day, if people are not engaged, they have choices. Patients have choices too. Patients are savvier now, and with greater ease of getting scorecards and information, they are going to make different choices. I would urge health care leaders to understand that patients going

forward will have more choice than ever, and it is best to serve our patients with a group of people that are dedicated and engaged. What we're asking you to do, as one of those leaders, is to examine the way you lead, and to help determine ways to truly engage those people in your own organization in order to produce better results for your patients.

INTRODUCING THE AUTHORS

So who are we anyway, and why should you care what we have to say about anything? Well, Paul Spiegelman is cofounder and CEO of The Beryl Companies, a patient experience service and thought leadership organization located in Dallas, Texas. BerylHealth helps hospitals improve patient interactions, and The Beryl Institute publishes research that validates the connection between improving the patient experience and driving better clinical and financial outcomes. And Britt Berrett (former CEO of Medical City Dallas Hospital) is currently president of nine-hundred-bed Texas Health Presbyterian Hospital, also in Dallas. Both organizations are in industry segments (Paul runs a call center, and Britt runs a hospital) known for low morale, high attrition, and low margins. Yet we've achieved not only results related to employee and customer service (including industry-leading metrics for employee loyalty and retention) but also financial results well in excess of our competitors. Plus, our organizations have won multiple local, regional, and national Best Place to Work awards, which should tell you that we know a thing or two about building the kind of organizational culture where employees thrive.

"But wait," you're probably saying, "you guys run two completely different kinds of organizations. Aren't there going to be some major differences between what one of you does as a hospital administrator and what the other does as owner of a small business?" You make a great point. There's no doubt that Britt faces different operational and strategic challenges from those Paul faces. Where Britt has to keep on top of the latest changes in the health care system emanating from Capitol Hill, for instance, Paul spends time contemplating the merits of bringing in outside capital to help grow his company. But our point is that you can boil down the secret of success to one idea: If you build a great culture for you and your people to work in, it doesn't matter what kind of organization you work in or for. Whether you're guiding a public company toward financial results or leading a small, entrepreneurial company that has no outside influences, the same employee engagement methods lead to better results, in terms of both generating better customer experiences and driving improved financial metrics.

That's why, after hitting it off at an industry conference about the importance of fostering a strong corporate culture, we remained friends and eventually kindled the idea that we needed to boil down our experiences into this book. While we don't pretend to know everything there is about the subject, we did our best to share our lessons learned with you—beginning in the next chapter, where we'll cover the subject of leadership and how what it means to be a leader has changed in recent years. In the chapters that follow, we'll also tackle subjects such as the importance of embracing your organization's mission, vision, and values; why having fun—and creating smiles—is mission critical, especially for health care organizations; and why showing people that you really care about them, both inside and outside of the walls of your organization, helps fuel future success. We'll also talk about how you'll need to say good-bye to those people in your organization who refuse to buy into the mission, vision, and values, so you can spend your time recognizing and rewarding those employees who "get it." In our final chapter, we'll share our thoughts about what we like to call our "higher power": the guiding light that drives us to embrace the lessons of this book not only because it makes good business sense, but more important, because it's the right thing to do. As a bonus, we've also included a tool of sorts so you can test how your organization ranks in terms of Culture IQ™, or CIQ—a tool we've devised to help measure how well your culture is built to drive employee engagement.

Building the kind of organizational culture where everyone thrives is a shared passion of ours, and our goal in writing this book is nothing less than changing the entire U.S. health care system along these lines. Look, there's a crisis going on in health care, and everyone is looking in the wrong places for a cure. Let's face it: The times they are a-changing, and you're going to need backup. As Elliot Joseph, CEO of Hartford Healthcare in Hartford, Connecticut, told us:

> There is a reason why so many soap operas are set in hospitals: because they're just petri dishes of exciting and interesting and intriguing drama every day. I like to say you can

stand outside the front of one of our hospitals and you will see every emotion known to mankind in one day.

When it comes to making changes in environments like these, it's not just about getting people to do better, to behave differently, to do what they're currently doing in a nicer and better and more efficient manner. That's not even half the battle. The other piece of it is that without an engaged, satisfied—I want to say "excited," but that's probably not the right word—workforce that's capable of change management and changing the way we do things, we can't succeed. Because this industry is broken. The idea of change management in an environment of low morale and disengagement—from my point of view, it is almost an impossible task.

The outlook may sound grim, but we, like Elliot Joseph, have come to learn the secret to successfully changing how an organization can operate at its best. By reading this book, you'll learn it too.

Okay, so that sounds a bit ambitious for just two guys from Texas, but we believe we're up to the challenge. Are you? And you don't have to believe just us—we personally interviewed dozens of CEOs from some of the most prestigious hospital and health care systems across the United States, some of whom you already met in this chapter. Throughout our book, we've included their thoughts and advice about building an engaged workforce. Are you curious as to what they told us? Follow us to the next chapter, and you'll find out.

CHAPTER TWO

Changing How We Lead

The words *puerperal fever* might not raise the hairs on the back of your neck the way, say, the term *avian flu* does these days. But for more than two centuries, the disease was a rampant, insidious killer in Western hospitals, targeting mothers of newborn children and often threatening to turn those cherubic babies into motherless orphans just days after their birth. The origin of the fever—and its cure—remained a mystery until the early nineteenth century, when a Hungarian physician named Ignaz Semmelweis discovered the cause: dirty hands.

What initially puzzled Semmelweis was the fact that among women who gave birth at home, the fever was contracted far less often than among those who were admitted to the hospital maternity ward. After studying the differences in the two environments, Semmelweis came to realize that the sickness was spread because doctors refused to wash their hands. This had something to do with an archaic attitude of the time; in the words of Dr. Charles Meigs, a leading obstetrician in eighteenth-century Philadelphia, "Doctors are gentlemen, and a gentleman's hands are always clean." But Semmelweis found that when doctors simply washed their hands with an antiseptic solution before visiting their patients, the mortality rate for new mothers dropped from 35 percent to less than 1 percent. Unfortunately for the good doctor (and for innumerable patients of the era), his peers derided his findings, which Semmelweis published in the book *Etiology, Concept, and Prophylaxis of Childbed Fever*. It was only after his premature death at the age of forty-seven that his findings gained traction, helped largely by Louis Pasteur's research on germs.

Today, of course, even young children are taught to wash their hands regularly to prevent the spread of everything from the flu to the common cold. But that doesn't mean everyone likes to be told to do it. Even in modern hospitals, which rely on sterile environments and the latest advances in medical technology, we still stress that everyone should wash his or her hands. No, check that: We directly order everyone to wash his or her hands.

The problem is, it's still a problem. People still don't wash their hands. You can almost imagine Semmelweis rolling over in his grave, wondering aloud, "What the heck is going on?" That's why many hospitals have experimented with ways to get the message out to nurses and orderlies, trying everything from handing out bonus checks for 100 percent compliance to installing antiseptic foam dispensers on the door of every room in the building. And still it's not enough to get everyone on board.

Strangely enough, the hospital departments that have had the highest degree of success in getting workers to wash their hands are the ones that don't try to enforce a rule or come up with some kind of gimmick like giving out bonuses or putting up posters. Instead they engage their workers in a conversation about personal values and health care work as a calling. Rather than just tell them what they need to do, the leaders who achieve the best results explain why hand washing is so important. They simply emphasize that dirty hands are injuring patients and putting them directly into harm's way, and this message resonates with people who have chosen to work in a sector whose overarching goal is to help people. It is only by connecting with employees' values in this way that hospital leaders can actually lead their employees toward positive change.

RETHINK THE LEADER'S ROLE

We use the hand washing story to illustrate the cultural sea change that has occurred around the notion of what it means to be a leader. When you think of great leaders, perhaps images of fierce military leaders like Julius Caesar and Genghis Khan come to mind—men who fought on the front lines and ruled by force. Any follower so bold as to second-guess an order, let alone disregard it, could count on some serious pain as a consequence. Or perhaps you think of influential politicians like John F. Kennedy and Ronald Reagan, men who employed enormous charm and charisma to inspire action. Once you gazed into such a leader's eyes, or heard him give a glorious speech, you might be inspired to tackle something new all on your own. Then again, maybe the term *leader* makes you think of your boss, the person who fills out your annual performance review and signs your paycheck every two weeks.

There might not be anything personally compelling about your boss, other than that he or she sits higher than you on your organization's hierarchical tree. Your job is simply to follow this "leader's" orders.

Researchers have given different names to different styles of leadership over the years, but for now we'd like to focus on this last idea, this notion of following orders, known as the command-and-control or transactional model of leadership. There's good reason that this style of leadership has flourished in recent history, especially in sectors like the military or manufacturing, where the system or the process gets more emphasis than the individual. But we're here to tell you that all this has changed—big-time. A combination of factors, including the aging of the baby boomers and the rise of the millennial generation, has caused the gradual decline of the command-and-control style of leadership. It's no longer good enough just to tell a subordinate to do something. Today, leadership means explaining why following that order matters—or better yet, empowering subordinates themselves to make the best decisions for the good of the organization as a whole.

This is what biographer and scholar James MacGregor Burns (in his book *Transforming Leadership*) dubbed transformational leadership, saying that "transforming leaders champion and inspire followers . . . [so that] they might become leaders themselves." Or, as Jay Alden Conger and Rabindra Nath Kanungo put it in their book, *Charismatic Leadership in Organizations*, transformational leaders "are able to motivate subordinates to [higher] levels of performance . . . by raising the importance of certain goals, by

demonstrating the means to achieve them, and by induc-
ing subordinates to transcend their self-interests" for the
achievement of organizational goals.

Even the military has recognized the need to change
along these lines. Take Seal Team Six, the U.S. Navy's Special Forces unit that ultimately hunted down and elimi-
nated Osama Bin Laden. While members of the team have
hierarchical ranks, each member is actually trained to perform the job of everyone else on the team—just in case, as it
always does, the situation on the battlefield breaks down.
Consider what happened when Seal Team Six dropped in
on Bin Laden's compound, only to have one of its helicop-
ters crash. That obviously wasn't part of the plan. And
while the team likely had trained for such a contingency, it
also had empowered its members to make snap decisions in
the moment rather than waiting until they received orders
from higher-ups. Each member of the team knew the ultimate goal of their shared mission, and each had the tools
required to make sure that goal was accomplished. What
the military has come to realize is that when you turn your
employees into drones who don't act until they are told to
act, your whole organization can quickly become paralyzed,
often when it can least afford to be.

Today's best business leaders have come to understand
the same principle: that they can get the best results when
they engage their subordinates in the mission, vision,
and values of their organization. The word *engagement*
is a funny descriptive word that means more than just
"understanding"; it is transitional, meaning we are taking an individual or a team from one state of "being" to

another. Engagement means we move from understanding a concept in a sterile and impersonal way to embracing it with the very fiber of our soul. We become engaged not just because we understand the science behind a concept, but because we really, truly get it. Gary Newsome, CEO of Health Management Associates in Naples, Florida, framed it like this:

> The culture of an individual hospital relies heavily on the leadership team of that hospital. The tone has to be set at the top. Everyone needs to understand: What is the goal? How are we going to get there? Every individual, from nursing to dietary to housekeeping to business ops, has to have a common understanding.

Think back to our story about hand washing, where we learned that simply giving orders didn't change anyone's behavior. It was only when leaders connected with employees' sense of inner purpose that the nurses and orderlies began to truly understand the significance of washing their hands regularly. Again, the act of leading is no longer about simply issuing orders. It's about finding a way to inspire people to act in purposeful and meaningful ways. It's about everyone feeling as though what he or she does can make a difference.

His organization's mission, vision, and values are so important to Alan Channing, CEO of Sinai Health in Chicago, that he personally teaches them to every new associate on his or her first day, to provide the context for why such things matter:

I finish my talk by making two promises, and I tell them these are the only two promises I can deliver on. The first is that you'll be frustrated. You'll hear a decision, not know what it means, et cetera. The other promise is that you will be able to make a difference in someone else's life. So when you're feeling the effects of that first promise, remember the second. It is really fun for me to engage in this conversation. I see the light go on in their eyes.

Seeing that "light" in their eyes is how you'll know that you're on the right path as a leader—that you are connecting with and inspiring your people.

ENGAGE EMPLOYEES WITH A HIGHER PURPOSE

Have you ever heard of *kaizen*, the Japanese concept of taking incremental steps toward success? We read an apt story in a book devoted to this philosophy and process of improvement, and it ties this whole topic together quite nicely. The story centers around a ten-doctor medical group in the United States that was experiencing tremendous problems with patient satisfaction. Wanting to get to the bottom of the problem, the group surveyed its customers and learned that long wait times was the number one complaint from their patients. In an effort to address that problem, the group's leadership went to their playbook for answers. First, they hired a few more doctors, thinking that would cut down on those wait times. It didn't work. In fact, patients somehow grew less satisfied.

The group's leaders then invested in new scheduling software to help them spread out their appointments better. But even that did little to improve patient satisfaction scores. It seemed that no matter what changes the medical group's leaders made, it only further confounded the problem.

The answer to the dilemma ultimately came not from the group's leadership, but from the staff. And the changes they implemented didn't cost a dime. Their solution? The staff simply informed patients as soon as they showed up at the office about the expected wait time and apologized if things were running behind schedule. But they didn't stop there. When the patient was finally shown in to an exam room, the first thing the doctor did was apologize for the long wait. Then, as the patient left the exam room, the receptionist would not only apologize again for the wait but also offer to schedule the patient's next appointment and thank the patient for coming in.

The results were spectacular; patient satisfaction scores soared. It turns out the wait times weren't the true issue. Patients expected to wait at the doctor's office! It was the unknown, and the apparent lack of concern, that drove them crazy. Simple as it was, the solution didn't arise until the group's leaders were willing to put aside their preconceived notions of what would work, like jiggering with the schedule or adding more doctors, allowing everyone to refocus on what truly drives the patient experience. The leaders had to put aside their ego and ask for help from the folks on the front lines—something many traditional leaders would rather jump off a cliff than do.

Unfortunately, most businesses, including most health care organizations, didn't get the memo about how leadership has evolved. Most leaders today continue to operate with blinders on, refusing to acknowledge the changes we've been discussing. The result is that they still employ the old command-and-control model perfected by a Roman general more than two thousand years ago. In our experience, most leaders today still don't trust subordinates to do anything more than what they've been ordered to do, and they still don't recognize how damaging that mind-set can be.

To be fair, we sympathize: It can be quite scary to give up the notion of control—especially when people's lives are at stake. As a leader in the health care field, you may be tempted to rely on checklists as a safeguard. But think about this analogy: Airline pilots also have checklists they walk through before every flight, making sure everything is in working order, from the landing gear to the ailerons (which control the up and down movement of the plane during flight). These pilots understand the purpose behind that checklist, however, which is to deliver their passengers safely to their destination. So when something looks wrong, even if it is not on the checklist, the pilot has the ability to act on it. Don't you want or expect the same from a nurse or orderly? You have given them the necessary tools and training to do their job. Shouldn't you rely on their engagement and creativity to fulfill the duties of the job as described by the checklist—but then also to go beyond that checklist to tackle the unanticipated issues that pop up?

We've said it before, but it's worth repeating: It simply is not enough to tell today's workers what to do or try to trick them into doing things with some kind of financial incentive. Generation Xers and millennials are not driven by financial rewards alone. They seek employment and careers that inspire them and tap their creativity. If they don't find that fulfillment in your organization, they will seek it elsewhere. The loyalty of the past has been replaced by the impetus to join a winning team, even if workers might give something up in the process. If your workforce isn't connecting to something bigger, if you're not offering up something more than "just a job," you won't hold on to your best people.

The most effective brand of leadership these days, then, is one that engages employees with a higher purpose—as defined by your organization's mission, vision, and values—in order for everyone to win. This practice of transformational leadership—what we have also begun to call purposeful leadership, holds true in any industry, including health care. The truth is, you need to change how you lead along these very lines. And you need to do it right now.

EMBRACE YOUR ORGANIZATION'S MISSION, VISION, AND VALUES

If you're still with us and you want to know how to start practicing what we've been preaching about—if you want to learn how you, too, can create a purpose-driven organization—please read on.

Let's begin by defining the relevant terms. In our parlance, we express the key building blocks of transformational leadership as follows:

- Mission: Why we are here
- Vision: Where we aspire to go
- Values: The rules we live by

Pretty straightforward, right? Well, while these may seem like commonsensical concepts, we admit that we both struggled to some degree as we went about implementing them in our own organizations.

When Britt began working at Medical City in Dallas, for example, the hospital had no mission statement, let alone a definition of its vision or values. But there was at least a recognition among the leadership and staff that everyone wanted to document the hospital's purpose—the reason they were all working there. At that time, creating a mission statement for an organization was somewhat of a craze du jour. Within the available management literature, there was no shortage of tips to choose from. Despite that, crafting a mission statement was an excruciating process for the team, partly because each individual had a different take on the three critical questions: Why are we here? Where are we going? What rules do we live by?

The key to success, in the end, is to personalize the mission, vision, and values statements so they have meaning for all stakeholders. And not just by creating something that can be recited—rather, you need to come up with something that is understood deeply and felt truly. Articulating the statements is an important process that, nevertheless, most everyone loathes. But doing so forces everyone to ask the most fundamental questions about their own role: Why am I here? Where do I want to go? What are my personal values? By talking through and personalizing the answers to these questions, individuals can begin to engage in the greater good for the team and the organization. As Dane Peterson, CEO of Emory University Hospital Midtown, told us:

> The overarching mission of a health care organization is an easy one to communicate—most employees and physicians choose their profession based on the mission. Everyone wants to be a part of something bigger than themselves, so even those employees who work in roles that are not found only in health care, and even those of us who came to health care later in life, can get excited about making a real difference in the lives of others.
>
> One key for leadership to remember is to avoid mixing messages around the mission. If leadership states one thing—best patient care, for instance—and then makes all its decisions based on financials, the employees will see this and become disengaged from the stated mission. Actions speak more forcibly than words, and when actions and words are aligned, engagement will follow.

Developing shared goals is the important thing, not just coming up with empty, meaningless statements.

By the same token, how many values your organization has is far less important than the fact that the values you choose must reflect what your employees actually believe in. This is not an exercise in simply handing down a mission, a vision, and values from atop Mount CEO. You need to make the time and effort to get everyone in your organization involved in setting those destinations—and in setting off on the journey to reach them. As Steve Rector, CEO at Regional Medical Center Bayonet Point in Hudson, Florida, put it for us:

> I've learned from my past experiences that it's very diffi-cult to get a group of individuals to read a statement, no matter how well written and inspirational it may be, much less to adopt it and then live it. It's our duty as leaders to engage the staff at a level at which we find out what that mission statement means to them. When they read it, what thoughts, visions, memories of their own lives come to mind? That's when it's no longer words; it's a personal connection that we then must help them live out in our organization.

Britt's colleagues at Medical City were mainly folks drawn to a higher calling in serving their fellow citizens, and still they struggled to develop a shared mission. Paul's experience in driving a mission statement through his organization (BerylHealth) was, if anything, even more painful, because while his business caters to the health care community, it's not a hospital. Paul's employees, as we mentioned, work in the call-center business—infamous for its "boiler room" environments. For the first few years that he operated the business, Paul admits he was a cynic; he didn't think anyone had a mission in showing up for work, and he didn't see the point in trying to establish one. But in time, helped by the wise words of a mentor, he came to see the light and got down to the task at hand.

To accomplish this goal, Paul created cross-functional teams within the organization. Only after several head-to-head meetings were they eventually able to bridge the chasm in terms of answering those same three key questions about the company's mission, vision, and values. In the end, BerylHealth decided on a simple, straightforward mission: Connecting people to health care. From that point on, BerylHealth has thrived, because it is able to focus on the key drivers of its growth rather than chase the smoke-and-mirror opportunities associated with more traditional telemarketing or sales activities, which could have caused the business to go off the track. Even better, the turnover rate at BerylHealth has dropped dramatically because, unlike most other call centers around the world, the people working there now have a defined purpose. And they even have a name: not agents, not customer service reps, but patient experience advocates. The people at BerylHealth know their purpose, and that is a beautiful thing.

Of course, you also have to be wary of drinking too heavily of your own Kool-Aid, which is why it's very important to bring objective results into the mix every now and then. Making sure your team is on track with its purpose is critical. Britt recalls an instance when things went awry at Medical City even though the hospital staff had its mission statement to guide them. A patient survey had returned some particularly unsavory results; some of the patients had made intensely personal and derogatory comments about some of the nurses who had served them. When hospital leadership shared the results, the place, as you might expect, erupted. Accusations began flying, with some of the nurses even going so far as to say the results were made up. They weren't, of course, so in time, the nurses and the managers were able to move past their emotional reaction to focus on the results. They were able to actually look themselves in the mirror and see how they had strayed from their mission—admittedly, not an easy thing to do, but an essential one.

The truth is, even when you make the effort to construct your mission, values, and vision, it's likely that not everyone in the organization will buy into it. For example, several years ago Britt was meeting with his division president and chief financial officer in the hospital boardroom to explain plans for the future as part of their annual budgeting process. In his presentation, Britt continually referenced the organization's focus on the patient experience and how various tactics and strategies would translate into phenomenal results. Then, right in the middle of the presentation, the division CFO locked eyes with Britt and yelled, "You guys don't get it! This is a business!"

While Britt admits he was somewhat taken aback by the CFO's abruptness, he also couldn't help notice that hanging on the wall directly behind the CFO was the hospital's mission, vision, and values. You see, it is easy to put a plaque on a wall, but it's more difficult to have a profound understanding of the organization's mission and vision and values. Yup, it means more than a plaque. It should mean something to each and every individual . . . even the suits and ties!

Britt smiles when he retells the story, but the sad truth is that sometimes we can forget the larger context of what we're trying to do at work. There is no doubt hospitals are a business and need to make money to survive. But most people don't yet understand the link between running a values-based, mission-driven organization and how that positively drives financial performance. When employees are drawn to a purpose, they work harder because they feel connected to something bigger. It's no longer "just a job." They love what they do, and the customer—in our case, the patient—can feel the difference. Then, to complete the equation, when the customer is satisfied, financial performance improves.

You don't have to take our word for it. Just ask Tony Armada, CEO of Advocate Lutheran General Hospital, who put it this way:

> A mentor of mine once shared a very simple equation with me: If employees and physicians are happy, you'll get an increase in patient volume. If you increase volume, you'll find ways to decrease cost. With that, you'll increase margin and be able to invest back in employees.

This personally rewarding, profitable cycle makes perfect sense to us! At BerylHealth, we call it the Circle of Growth™. Simply put, if you invest in employee loyalty, customer loyalty will follow. If your customers are loyal, it will drive profits into your business. Now you can invest those profits back into your people, giving them better tools and resources to do their jobs. And the cycle repeats.

Of course, there are times when you need to confront those employees who fail to buy into the mission, vision, and values of the organization. Obviously, this happens to varying degrees, but it's an important issue and we'll address it in far more detail later on, particularly in chapter six. Not everyone will become instantly engaged in the company's ultimate goals, but when you do inspire engagement, you'll know it. The result is magical. Steve Rector, CEO at Regional Medical Center Bayonet Point, described it this way:

> I think leaders sometimes mistake someone who has a good attitude or personality for an engaged staff member. Be careful not to jump on that bandwagon. For me, it's fairly easy to notice engaged staff. They are usually the ones who are coming up to you in the hallway, the cafeteria, your office—wherever!—and providing insight on how you can improve, grow, do things better for the patients. It's not that they are smiling and happy all the time. In fact, sometimes they can be a little grumpy because they are so eager for improvement. But they always strive for improving the patient experience and challenge you as a leader to get engaged at every level to improve all things that touch the patient. I love these guys!

And so do we.

WHY INSPIRING YOUR EMPLOYEES MATTERS

Employee engagement doesn't happen overnight; it develops gradually and requires purposeful, continual encouragement and a flexible approach. As your organization and its people evolve over time, so can its values. At

BerylHealth, for instance, several additional values were added in recent years to help address a weakness or a need within the organization—namely, a spirit of camaraderie and a commitment to accountability. Those values are not just printed up and hidden behind a cheap frame that is hung in the lunchroom, though. The company's values are painted in four-foot-tall letters on the interior walls of the building. They're not easy to miss—or to forget.

Revisiting your values is also a vital exercise in coming back to the organization's purpose as a way to give it the weight it deserves. Knox Singleton has embraced change as CEO of Inova Health System in Falls Church, Virginia, and framed the evolving situation in today's health care organizations in the following way:

> What employees really want is a process where they have the opportunity to have an effect on their environment. In other words, what they do matters—it changes or impacts things. And then, secondly, they want to do worthwhile work. They want to connect what they're doing to some purpose that's worth pursuing.

By returning again and again to the organization's values and purpose, you remind your people why their work matters and encourage them to continue evolving in the right direction.

Here's an example: At Texas Health Presbyterian, Britt not only begins each and every meeting he runs by sharing the hospital's mission, vision, and values, but he also takes time to read aloud letters written by patients who have acknowledged the hard work done by the staff—positive feedback that supports their purpose. This is the sort of approach today's leaders need to take—and of course, you don't do this with the tone that you might use to read the letter the DMV sent, reminding you that your car registration is due. You need to just about sing the purpose of your organization as a way to inspire those around you to believe that they, too, are headed to the promised land of professional satisfaction along with you.

This approach also means finding ways to celebrate those colleagues who exemplify your organization's values and who become leaders by example. And the more you can facilitate ways that those awards are bestowed through peer recognition rather than coming from further up the hierarchy, the more powerful they become. For instance, at Britt's hospital, each department can nominate another department for a values-based Traveling Trophy award; the winning department receives a trophy that it can proudly display for everyone to see. Paul's team at BerylHealth accomplishes a similar result through its PRIDE program (Peers Recognizing Individual Deeds of Excellence). The program encourages BerylHealth employees to recognize the deeds of their coworkers, especially in other departments, by nominating them via an intranet-based system. Winners then receive awards and recognition—things like gift certificates and preferred parking spots (not just one, but five: one for each of the winners of that quarter's PRIDE award). Both of us have also used cash prizes and naming standout employees to "all-star" teams. These are just some of the alternative ways to drive home the message that mission, vision, and values are not just words; they represent a higher calling, and those members of the organization who buy into them will find themselves rewarded. Let's pause for a minute and take a breath. We're sure some of you like what you're hearing. But we're realistic enough to know that some of you reading this might still be somewhat cynical about the whole concept and why it matters. "I just don't think employees care about this kind of thing," you might be saying. "All they want is their paycheck." Fortunately for you, we anticipated your somewhat jaded perspective on the subject and prepared a story just for you.

The setting is Medical City in Dallas, many years ago. At that time, the organization decided to tackle the question "Who are we?" This is a fundamental question that any individual or organization must ask of itself in the formation of a mission statement. The program's intent was to kick off a dialogue from the employees' point of view about who they were and why they were working there. Dragging a video camera around the hospital and asking questions like "Why do you work here?" or "What does this place mean to you?" creates quite a stir, but more important, it forces some pretty revealing dialogue. The end result was a forty-five-minute video highlighting interviews with different people from throughout the organization who spoke about their connection to the history and nature of Medical City. A copy of the video was given to every member of the staff as an extra Christmas gift.

That wasn't enough for Millie, a food and nutrition technician—someone who was working at the entry level of the organization. She asked for several extra copies that she could send to her family in Guatemala. Millie wanted to use the video to show her family back home how proud she was of what she and her colleagues did on a daily basis—to show them that working for this organization fulfilled her life's purpose of doing good work and helping people. This led to an epiphany for everyone involved: The mission of the organization doesn't stop at its four walls. In fact, it goes as far as Guatemala or wherever an individual's family and loved ones live, and perhaps even beyond. If that doesn't hit home, revealing how important having a mission and a purpose is, and how tightly connected mission and purpose are to the notion of transformational leadership, we don't know what else to tell you in order to convince you.

Whew! Epiphanies and inspiration and fulfilling your purpose—heavy stuff. Do you feel as though this chapter was a little too much like a management tome you'd find at the airport bookstore? Fortunately for you, we're about to liven things up a bit. Having fun at work is the topic of the next chapter. We'll meet you there.

CHAPTER THREE

Fun Matters

Splash!

Imagine that you, family in tow, are headed to your company's annual picnic. Maybe it has been a pretty good year for your company and there are plenty of reasons to celebrate. But rather than looking forward to the event, you're kind of blasé about the whole thing. It'll just be more of the same, you might say to yourself on your way to the park, with the top guns taking all the credit and leaving nothing but a few hot dogs and hamburgers for the rest of us. Your family isn't all that excited about attending either. Well, maybe the kids are excited—they can always find something to smile about. In fact, there they go, laughing and pointing at something already. And what's all that commotion about anyway?

Splash!

"Dad, look—somebody is in the dunk tank!"

The dunk tank?

Yes, the dunk tank. We'll explain in just a moment.

Everyone knows that health care is no laughing matter. After all, people's lives are at stake. Every decision made or action taken by a hospital worker can impact a patient for the rest of his or her life. That's why, when you enter a hospital and take a look at the faces of the folks working there, you'll likely see a lot more frowns, knotted brows, and even tears than you do smiles and laughs. Working in health care is a calling and a duty—no one ever said it's a barrel of laughs. When you talk to people who work at a hospital, you're likely to hear them say they love their job and there is purpose behind what they do. Wouldn't it be inspiring if their love and purpose evolved into fun and happiness?

So imagine the following scenario: A major hospital in the Dallas area recruits a new chief executive officer to come in and help modernize its approach to delivering health care. This guy is young (just thirty-six), but he has already graduated with a degree from a prestigious medical school and is on his way to earning a PhD. You'd be forgiven, then, for anticipating that this guy comes from an ivory tower—that he's going to be a bit heady and obnoxious, full of annoying, fanciful new ideas to whip the hospital into shape.

Sure enough, soon after this new CEO joins the staff, he helps orchestrate an organization-wide celebration intended to pump everyone up about their future and, at the same time, raise some money for a few local charities. Yes, that's right—the annual picnic we described earlier. This guy is probably just going to get up on stage and crow about all the big changes he's going to make, all of which will make my job harder, you're probably thinking. But to your surprise, as your kids just discovered, the main event of the celebration is the opportunity for you, your coworkers, and even the family members who tagged along to plunk this new hotshot executive, dressed in a suit and tie of his Sunday best, into a barrel of cold water.

"Step right up!" calls the barker. "Three throws for five dollars! Now's your chance to dunk the new guy!"

"Dunk the new executive?" you exclaim. "Sign me up!"

One . . . two . . . three throws. Did you miss? No problem—just march right up and hit that button with your bare hand. He won't mind!

Splash!

In this particular scenario, the dunking goes on for about four hours, with hundreds of people taking their turn to knock this particular executive down to a more manageable size. Afterward, when you see this guy walking around, chatting and shaking hands with just about everyone—all while his suit and tie continue to drip water everywhere—he doesn't seem like such a stuffed shirt anymore. Maybe, just maybe, you might even open yourself up and listen to what he has to say. And that's when the magic can begin.

If you haven't guessed by now who the star of this story is, we'll give you a hint: He's one of the guys who wrote this book. You know, the one who still runs a hospital today. And the point of the story, other than illustrating that one of us (Britt) has a less-than-dry sense of humor, is that the ability to laugh—especially at yourself—may be one of the most valuable and overlooked talents a person can have. And that applies to anyone who works in any business, but especially in a health care organization. Steve Rector of Regional Medical Center Bayonet Point put it well:

For me, the most important aspect of laughter is being able to laugh at yourself. Showing those around you that you know no one is perfect, including yourself, humanizes your leadership and puts others at ease. I can promise you this: No one makes more mistakes than I do. So I better be prepared to laugh . . .

"But how can that be?" you ask. "After all, you just said that health care is serious business." That's true—we work in a business where life and death often hang in the balance. So we have to find a way to relieve all that seriousness . . . with a smile.

THE IMPORTANCE OF A SMILE

In the health care field, where we work in the fray and often forget to take the time and effort to find the joy in what we do—and where we fail to see the humor that often comes along with our serious work—we can end up frying ourselves. We've seen it far too often, where talented and caring people simply burn out. Dane Peterson, CEO of Emory University Hospital Midtown, explained it this way:

I think laughter in the workplace is critical. Even in life-or-death institutions like hospitals, it is important to enjoy the work. If we cannot laugh and enjoy the good times, it is hard to handle the inevitable difficult times. We spend more time at work than we do with our families. Work that is drudgery doesn't create proper work–life balance and de-energizes employees.

If your own well-being isn't reason enough to let your sense of humor shine through, consider those whom you serve. Patients are hyperalert to their surroundings and the people tending to them. If they are forced to deal with deadly serious and stressed-out nurses, orderlies, and doctors all day long, how do you think they'll start to feel? Sure, there are times when you can go too far, and you need to be mindful of your limits. We refer to these guardrails as the "organizational values"—the beliefs that govern your actions both personally and collectively. But your values should never interfere with becoming a better person or organization, so finding ways to laugh at ourselves—even if you have to put yourself in the dunk tank to do so—can relieve some of that tension so omnipresent along hospital hallways. That's a notion that Bob Kelly, president of New York–Presbyterian Hospital, agrees with:

> My wife thinks I'm the most unfunny person in the world. But at the hospital, people actually think I've got a good sense of humor. I think you can find a way to smile and laugh in a lot of situations. Obviously it has to be done with dignity and respect; you can't make fun of patients or something like that. But even in the operating room, when the patient has gone to sleep, people can tell jokes, they can relax, they can sort of let down a little bit, and I think that's really important.

It's not that hospital workers have a monopoly on tense jobs. Let's face it: Not many of us would consider it fun to be on the phone all day with frustrated and upset customers, but that's all part of the job at a call center. Do you want to know one of the key reasons why BerylHealth, which operates in an industry with one of the highest turnover rates around, not only keeps its talent but also gets people knocking on the door to get hired? Because its CEO does strange things like dress up as Howie Mandel (joined by J.Lo, Steven Tyler, and Charlie Sheen) to host a company-wide *Gong Show*–themed talent show. On a workday! Or maybe it's because that same CEO once featured himself in a video documentary where he donned his pajamas and went out in search of a new career because, as the plot unfurled, BerylHealth had evolved to the point where he was no longer needed. In fact, it could be any number of things that Paul has done to keep things fun at Beryl-Health—from the time he starred in the movie *Small Paul*, where a six-inch version of himself explored the company, to the momentous occasion when he and other company leaders competed in a special version of *Dancing with the Stars*, called "Dancing with the Executives." The dancing might not have been all that elegant (actually, given the roller-skating matadors, it was downright goofy at times), but it served a purpose—it created camaraderie.

Think back to some of the best friends you've had in your life, and we'll bet you recall all the fun things you did together and bonded over: the vacations, the parties, maybe even the work outings. It seems we humans are wired to connect with one another when we're having fun. When you're doing something that brings a smile to your face, you're transported away from the normal worries that tend to consume you both at home and at the office.

When those neurons in your brain fire, releasing all those good endorphins throughout your body, you feel as though you've escaped on a vacation even though you're actually at work. In fact, when you feel that good, you're probably doing the best work you're capable of.

Still having a hard time believing that "the funny" can make such a difference? Take a turn working the night shift when we hold a contest to match pictures of new medical staff with famous movie stars. Or take the field in a softball game that pits the staff of the medical intensive care unit against the surgical intensive care unit. Believe us, it's funny to see these folks falling around the infield. And it's amazing how the teams bond along the way. These folks do serious stuff and work all hours of the day, and yet they find a way to crack a smile that leads into those full-belly laughs.

This connection between happy workers and engaged workers has attracted the attention of researchers because, quite frankly, we're living in a time where worker engagement ranks near all-time lows. According to a 2010 Gallup survey, about 30 percent of workers in the U.S. report being engaged in their jobs, while an astounding 70 percent say they basically couldn't care less about their choice of employment. Consider that figure for a moment: That means that more than two-thirds of the interactions you have on a daily basis—from eating lunch at your local deli to picking up your dry cleaning to choosing a data plan for your new iPhone—are with people who aren't engaged with their job. These are the people who just don't care. Oh, it's not like they are going to sabotage your experience (though there are plenty of videos out there on YouTube that show some despicable acts), but they don't really care about you or about the kind of interaction you're having with them.

So how do you get those 70 percent to see their jobs differently? Find something that will make their job more than bearable—something that will make it fun.

FINDING YOUR FUNNY BONE

Just because someone works in the health care field doesn't mean that he or she was born without a funny bone. In fact, when given the go-ahead to have fun, this person might be hilarious! Often you don't have to coax people out of their shell; you just need to give them permission to smile and to show off their funny side.

Many hospital workers won't give themselves permission to have fun, though, because they take their jobs perhaps too seriously. And for good reason: They do work that is serious. Even the architectural choices made when building hospitals—from the stark white of the corridors to the dark mahogany paneling of the administration offices—seem to demand reverence and silence. But that doesn't mean you can't find the right balance between fun and serious. Striking that balance often becomes a function of leadership at all levels of the organization. We have to not only give employees the okay to have fun at their jobs but also find ways to encourage it.

Now, we hear you: Your team and your closest friends are funny, but those other guys are a bunch of stiffs—and don't get us started on the physicians. But you're wrong. Everyone can bring out "the funny" at times. Try inviting it. To be sure, it can seem a little risky to have fun, kind of like telling a joke and having everyone just stare at you (cue the sound of crickets chirping in the background). To feel safe, start small. Take a chance at your next staff meeting or employee gathering. Find a coconspirator, and break from tradition. Announce a new award for excellence, and give out a ridiculous item or token prize to the winner (you'll learn more about our version of this, the Berrett's Carrot, in chapter eight). Or invent and dress up like a superhero—you could become Scorro, visiting staff meetings and congratulating the teams with the highest patient satisfaction scores. The possibilities are limitless, and the rewards outweigh the risks, especially when you keep in mind the purpose behind the madness.

Not every CEO or department head has to submit to the dunk tank, but it sure is an effective way to show that you're not just talking the talk. It is only when everyone, cafeteria workers and executives alike, engages in the spirit of having fun that the organization can move forward toward its ultimate goal: taking care of patients as best it can.

When we give permission to unleash "the funny," magic happens. Consider the administrative director who saw such a drop in his hospital's HCAHPS scores that he came up with the idea of a not-so-super hero named Mediocre Man and his trusty sidekick, the Apathetic Avenger. Complete with red tights and a camera to record their antics, these two characters travel through the hospital, celebrating exceptional results and spreading smiles and fun. You never know when or where they'll turn up—they can be seen in any department, on any shift! These two familiar figures have become icons, and it all started when we agreed that it is important to smile and have fun.

It's okay if you've started to sweat a bit after reading about antics such as dressing up like celebrities or subjecting yourself to public humiliation via the dunk tank. Everyone's sense of "fun" can be different. That means it shouldn't be an organization-wide mandate to participate in the company talent show (though it's interesting that most people will). We can even admit that the two of us, while bonding over a shared sense of humor, often express ourselves very differently. Take Paul, for example, who is a self-described introvert. As a child, he actually had to be reminded by his mom to smile—perhaps foretelling for a guy who grew up to write a book titled *Why Is Everyone Smiling?* He kind of keeps to himself when he's surrounded by people; it took a goofball movie like *Bridesmaids* to get Paul to laugh out loud on an airplane.

That's all to say that Paul shows his emotions differently than, say, Britt, an extrovert who not only allowed himself to be dunked but also has donned a Batman costume in the name of excellence in health care. It was a Brittman costume, actually. Accompanied by the Boy Blunder (a guy who just now happens to be the CEO of a prestigious hospital in Atlanta—we'll call him "Dane"), Brittman drove a scooter down the halls of a hospital ward on a mission to bring excellent patient experiences and service to every nook and cranny of the building.

The key point here is a serious one: While Britt sure had some fun living out a childhood fantasy as Brittman, he did it with a purpose. Paul didn't sit for three hours getting Howie Mandel makeup and a bald skullcap applied just for the heck of it. They did it to loosen everyone up and let their employees know that they, too, had permission to have some fun at work. We're not trying to take credit for coming up with these ideas. On the contrary, we readily admit that we stole them from other people. And others have stolen from us—like John Hill, CEO of Medical Center of Aurora in Denver, who once had his associate administrator dress up as Magnet Man, in a costume sporting a bright yellow leotard, a mask, and accompanying cape and shoes, to celebrate their hospital's recognition as an ANCC Magnet Recognition Program® hospital for nursing excellence, the highest honor for nursing quality. But as they say, imitation is the greatest form of flattery. The important idea here is the willingness to let your hair down, so to speak, as a way to encourage colleagues and associates to display their natural creativity. When you give employees a specific job to do, creativity can be stifled and, as a result, a person's natural talents are wasted. When you open up the possibilities for people to bring that creativity to work, however, fun and engagement ensue.

But remember, you really can't push funny. Everyone has her own favorite flavor, so sometimes all you can do is invite participation as a way to tease out "the funny" and see what personalities emerge. As John Hill put it, "People love to laugh. The best way to teach someone is to make them laugh first and then teach the desired principle or lesson."

Case in point: BerylHealth sponsored a daily activity as a way to celebrate National Customer Service Week. On

Friday of that week, every department was encouraged to choose a movie as a theme and dress up accordingly. Now, regardless of what kind of company or organization you work for, we think you'll agree that the IT department is often the most casual when it comes to the notion of "office attire." Generally speaking, they're not always the easiest people to engage with either (tech-speak is a whole other language, foreign to many of us). So we figured the IT team at BerylHealth might not be all that inspired to dress up. Wrong. The whole department threw themselves into it, making fun of themselves in the process by arriving at work dressed up as the team from *Revenge of the Nerds*, complete with hiked-up pants and Coke-bottle glasses. You should have been there—it was hilarious. But just as important, their stunt created bonds between members of the IT team and also brought down the barriers that existed between them and the rest of the company. Once you allow someone to have a laugh at your expense, that person is going to be more at ease and open to making connections with you. By poking fun at themselves, the IT team made themselves more approachable to the rest of the company, which made BerylHealth a better company in the process.

HOW HAVING FUN PAYS OFF

Okay, there might still be some skeptics reading along with us, wondering aloud about what our point is. "Sure, having fun at work sounds like a great idea," you might be saying, "but show me some results." Fair enough.

In order to "show you the money," let's do our best impression of the Ghost of Christmas Past and travel back a few years to when Britt first landed at Texas Health Presbyterian Hospital in Dallas. "Presby," as the locals affectionately call it, is a nine-hundred-bed facility that has earned local and national recognition. But behind the success, there were some disturbing indicators. First and foremost of these was its employee engagement score, which ranked Presby merely in the fiftieth percentile compared to hospitals across the country. Sure, it would have been easy to rest on our laurels and keep cruising along as we always had. Hey, we were doing an average job, and that ain't bad! But the leadership team decided that it wasn't good enough, especially when we recognized that there were changes afoot in terms of the HCAHPS measures and that the government would soon begin tying patient satisfaction scores to federal compensation for health care providers.

Since we believed there was a direct relationship between employee engagement and patient satisfaction scores, we threw ourselves into the effort of having some fun to tackle both concerns at once. The team at Presby began to hold a series of employee forums—internal gatherings where two hundred to three hundred employees were invited to discuss issues and ideas related to how we all could improve the patient experience. (The notion of communicating with employees and getting feedback from them is something we'll dig into deeper, in chapter seven.) After kicking off each one-hour meeting—to accommodate everyone's schedule, there were eighteen in total—we would go through the hospital's mission, vision, and values. Then we would launch into a discussion about our organizational goals.

We can hear you yawning; yadda, yadda, yadda, right? Figuring we might get such a reaction from the folks in the audience, we decided to do something crazy: We tried to make the meetings fun. How? Well, we produced and screened music videos, including ones featuring Mr. Bill and a homemade version of *Star Wars*. We gave out gifts and threw T-shirts out into the crowd. We even had the senior leaders dress up like Mexican banditos to change things up.

To make sure we learned as much as possible from each experience, we surveyed every attendee to see what he or she thought. The reaction was, unfortunately, somewhat predictable: Not everyone bought into it. Some people told us that since this wasn't something we had done in the past, it made them uncomfortable. Others were more blunt: They told us we were acting like sixth graders. We didn't even need a survey to gauge that some people disapproved; those from one department just sat in the audience with their arms folded, rolling their eyes at the antics onstage.

It would have been easy at this point to can the idea of having fun and just go back to doing what we'd always done. But that's where the element of professional risk comes into play. We had to place ourselves in the dunk tank in order to initiate the change we needed. Where we were was not where we wanted to be. What we were already doing wasn't going to take us to where we wanted to go.

Now, fast-forward to the following year. Over the twelve months that passed, we had developed new uniforms and dress codes; initiated the Midnight Munchies program (which you'll hear about in chapter four) and a system of daily rounding called the Sacred Sixty; and held celebrations and wild events in the main concourse, serving hundreds of pizzas and scooping gallons of ice cream. When the operating room team achieved exceptional results, we covered ourselves in plastic sheets and ponchos and showered them with Martinelli's Sparkling Cider! We showed that we listened to our people, and more than that, we cared what they were saying.

The results were amazing: In just one year, we improved our employee engagement score from the fiftieth percentile all the way to the eighty-first percentile—a massive improvement, to put it mildly. (For what it's worth, we're all the way up to the ninety-third percentile at the time of writing this book.) By introducing the employee forums— where we reviewed our shared purpose, listened to one another's concerns, and reminded everyone to have a little fun in the process—we demonstrated to employees that what they thought and did mattered, and they responded positively. We had taken a bit of a risk, but it paid off big-time.

When we surveyed our employees at the end of the forums once again we included one question: Did you have fun at the employee forum? We learned that 13 percent of our associates reported they didn't have any fun. That left 87 percent enjoying themselves. Not bad, right? What's interesting, though, is how that statistic correlated with the percentage of the workforce who also reported being actively disengaged at work: 13 percent. We don't think we need to hit you over the head for you to see the connection here. The people who don't have fun and the people who are disengaged at work are more than likely to be the same people! What this tells us is that as a leader, you might eventually be forced to make some tough decisions regarding personnel and recruiting as you try to find the right mix of employees who do buy into the idea of having fun at work—something we'll discuss further in chapter six.

CAN DOCTORS HAVE FUN?

The uncomfortable reality of tweaking staff brings us to a related and difficult subject: doctors. First off, here in the United States, we have the most highly skilled and intelligent physicians anywhere in the world. Unfortunately, there is a price to pay. While the rest of us are having the time of our lives in college and the like, would-be doctors hole themselves up in musty university libraries with their noses buried in textbooks for up to sixteen years. Sixteen years! When they emerge from their warrens as newly minted doctors, their word becomes law. The rub, of course, is that they are still the same intellectual brains who shunned the rest of us fun-seekers.

That's not to say that doctors can't be fun, however. Some of them are hilarious! But they have been trained and taught to be stoic and serious. There is the rare exception, of course—like Patch Adams, played by Robin Williams in the movie of the same name. But even Patch couldn't always hit the funny bone quite right.

Physicians can be our greatest allies in considering the patient's experience, because we are striving to help care for their patients. Their dedication and commitment to each patient is very real and personal, and that makes them a great teammate in our shared endeavor. But physicians can also be proud individuals who might never have learned how to let down their guard or even how to truly function as a member of a team. That can make physicians difficult to work with from the perspective of the rest of a hospital's staff. In fact, there is even a website (www.stop bullyingnurses.com) that speaks to this very problem. It states that some 90 percent of nurses have reported being verbally abused—yelled at or insulted—most often by a physician. That's part of why doctors often get a reputation as not always being the friendliest people you'll ever meet.

That said, for every memorable jerk there is an entire staff of wonderful and caring physicians. Yes, we tend to always remember the jerks. But when you take a look at all the other quiet and caring physician warriors who are part of the team—those people who want the very best for their patients, and who let it show—you begin to see how much a positive patient experience means to them.

Given all that, we think you'd agree that getting doctors to embrace the concept of having fun at work might be a difficult challenge. We won't lie: It is. That means we as leaders need to keep finding ways for these highly skilled people to take off their white lab coats, ask people to call them by their first name (seriously, no one calls us "Attorney Spiegelman" or "Chief Executive Berrett," do they?), and take a chance by laughing at themselves.

When you can engage physicians through a bit of mischief-making, as we said before, magic happens. One of the all-time classic videos produced at Presby featured a group of physicians performing the Beach Boys' "Surfin' USA" in an operating room—hysterical! At Medical City, we had a harder time convincing doctors to let down their guard. A group of docs were asked to film a video tied to the Van Halen song "Jump," where these doctors would "jump" out of various locations in time with the music. The purpose of the video was to highlight the importance of "jumping" to complete their medical records! Lame? Absolutely! It was hilarious, though, and when we developed the idea it seemed that everyone was excited. But when we asked the group of fifteen physicians to participate, you could see them looking at one another out of the corner of their eyes, to see if someone would flinch. The idea may have sounded great to them, but we hadn't accounted for group norming and the power of peer pressure. They wanted to do it—we could almost see the budding excitement—but they had adopted this kind of groupthink: I am a doctor and a life giver. I need to be serious.

It wasn't until we cornered each physician on an individual basis that the sparks began to fly and the video took on a life of its own. Once we got the ball rolling by persuading the medical staff president to jump out from behind a desk, we knew we had ignited a fire at last. Soon, docs began jumping out from just about everywhere. Each attempted to outdo the last. Eventually we had to put a stop to the free-flowing creativity, or one of the docs would have ended up with a broken hip.

Can you see the power of what can happen when leadership establishes a culture that encourages fun? Admittedly, we aren't all the way there yet; many physicians remain uncomfortable with the notion of having fun. The good news, though, is that there is hope on the horizon in the form of physicians from the millennial generation now graduating from medical school. These millennials are still studying for the better part of a decade or two, but they've probably spent more time in study groups than their bookish counterparts of past generations did. They've grown up working in teams, thanks to the evolving focus on transformational leadership, so they understand how group dynamics work. In fact, some hospitals have begun to recruit doctors out of medical school as much for their interpersonal and collaborative skills as for their technical acumen—something that was unheard of in the past. For example, Ron Swinfard, CEO of Lehigh Valley Health System, told us about how his organization has forged a partnership with the University of South Florida to help identify medical students who are particularly empathetic and compassionate—characteristics that his hospital values in the physicians it hires.

These future docs are entering a field that has grown infinitely more complex over the years. Physicians twenty years ago needed to understand something like seven different drugs. By our count, today that number is in the hundreds when you add up all the drugs that lower cholesterol, blood pressure, and whatnot. Docs now must surf a tsunami of information—which means no one person can do it all anymore. It's a new era that involves working on cross-disciplinary teams with pharmacists, dieticians, and nurse practitioners. It used to be that every physician wanted to hang a shingle and go into business for him- or herself. But the new guys and gals say they don't want to do it alone. They want to be part of a team—something bigger than themselves. Maybe, just maybe, these newly minted docs will also be willing to crack a smile at a joke every now and then. If so, it will be a good day for everyone.

WHY FUN MATTERS

Before we move on, let's go back to the point about why having fun matters: It ultimately helps improve our patients' experiences. That's why we're here, after all. If we as leaders can put together a staff of nurses, orderlies, and physicians who can relax and let down their guard, who can act like (gulp!) real, honest-to-goodness human beings now and again, we'll find ourselves on the right track. That means we can also find ways to have fun while engaging with our patients.

Let's say you walk into your local hospital, stroll across the lobby, and hit the elevator button for your physician's floor. Imagine your surprise when the elevator door opens to let you in, and there's a guy in a suit sitting there at a desk. "Hello! Welcome to the elevator!" he exclaims. Well, if you hadn't run away in confusion, you'd have learned that it was in fact the hospital's chief executive—Britt—seated there in the elevator with you.

This really happened. Why? The desk stunt served as an example for every hospital worker to begin thinking differently about the time they spend in the elevators. You know how it is: Everyone pretends not to be looking at one another, and an uncomfortable silence seems to coat everything. That's not a great way for patients or their families to begin their hospital experience. By doing something unusual and (hopefully) somewhat amusing, Britt and his team attempted to enhance the patient experience not only directly, by getting patients to smile, but also indirectly, by encouraging everyone to reach out and connect with patients (and coworkers, for that matter) wherever and whenever they can. Once again, the point was to use fun as a way to build momentum toward our ultimate goal: improving the patient experience.

As health care leaders, we can also extend the idea of having fun to our families and our communities. For example, every year on the day before Halloween, BerylHealth—which is housed in an old Walmart building the size of a small neighborhood—basically closes up shop for a day so everyone's kids can come trick-or-treating around the cubicles. At other times throughout the year, the company hosts carnivals in its parking lot. It even invests in producing a monthly magazine called *Beryl Life*, which includes stories about the company along with creative craft projects for families to tackle together at home. In other words, the idea of having fun at work doesn't stop when you sign off for the day: You bring it with you everywhere you go.

Getting in the dunk tank, so to speak, is a purposeful decision. It's not always easy, but it sure is worthwhile. We'll warn you, though, that regardless of what you do, you're going to run into detractors—people who will never buy in. But we're here to tell you that the risk is worth the reward: Giving people the permission to have fun at work—even when they do serious work like providing health care—creates phenomenal results. Not only will your patients enjoy their experience more, but (we dare say) your associates will enjoy their jobs more as well. What's not to like about that combination?

In the next chapter, we'll talk more about what it means to show your employees that you're thinking about not just patients but also the employees, their families, and the greater community—and that you really do care.

CHAPTER FOUR

Do We Really Care?

Working the graveyard shift at a hospital is hard work. Not only do you have to confront the inevitable challenging and life-threatening cases that come in through the ER, but you also have to manage your life away from work in what can seem like an upside-down world. Spending time with loved ones can seem like a thing of the past; it's frustrating when your spouse and kids are heading out the door in the morning, right when you're coming home to grab some sleep. It's also easy to feel forgotten and unappreciated, since most of the hospital executives stick to more traditional nine-to-five working days. How are they supposed to know whether nightshift employees are doing a good job or not when they're not even there? When you add all that up, it's easy to feel a bit disenchanted with your job.

Imagine, then, that you are a nurse in charge of the midnight shift of the burn unit, or maybe even a security guard whose duty is to scrutinize every character walking in and out of the building. Now picture this: A middle-aged guy with a big, goofy smile on his face is pushing a gigantic tray of cookies through the hallways on a gurney. This guy—who looks an awful lot like the hospital's chief executive—stops by to offer you one of those cookies.

"We've got chocolate chip, oatmeal raisin, sugar cookies
with sprinkles . . . Take your pick!" he says. Then he takes
a few minutes to stop and chat, asking you about how your
shift is going and whether there is anything he could do
to help.

As you chomp away on your delicious treat, you can't
help but smile back at this strange guy and tell him the
truth: both the good and the bad. And you know what, he
seems to be actually listening. "I'll see what I can do about
that," he says regarding one of your concerns. Then, after
shaking your hand, patting you on the back, or even giving you a hug, he's off—but not before saying, "You know
what? I really appreciate what you're doing." And you know
what? You actually believe him.

START WITH THE HEART

If we're being honest, most of us would admit to being a bit
cynical when it comes to work. When we hear our employer
say he or she is going to do this or that, we roll our eyes,
thinking, Yeah, right—I'll believe it when I see it. It's
even worse when your employer says something like "We
really care about you" or "We couldn't do it without you."
Whatever, man—just sign my paycheck, is probably what
you're thinking.

But wouldn't it blow your mind if in fact your employer
actually meant what he or she said about caring? What if—
gasp!—your boss even seemed to truly want to know how
your family was doing? Do you think that would change

how you feel not only about your boss but also about your entire work environment?

The point is, we can talk all we want about having a strong mission, vision, and values, and yes, it's crucial that we give permission for people to have fun at work. But if we as leaders and colleagues don't actually give a darn about the people we work with, all we've done is prove the cynics right. All we've shown them is that we talk the talk, but we don't walk the walk. When we do more than talk—when we demonstrate that we care about our people in the totality of their lives—those same people become infinitely more engaged in their jobs. The question, then, is this: Can you teach someone to actually care?

But first, what does it mean to "care"? To us, caring is a very important word that connotes love, kindness, and compassion. And it's our belief that just about everyone demonstrates that they care, in many ways throughout the day—whether that comes from caring for your family members, for your coworkers, or for the patients assigned to your ward. Here's how Ron Swinfard, CEO of Lehigh Valley Health System, put it:

> I participate in every new employee orientation. I use a presentation to show people my background, the one-room schoolhouse where I went to school. The slide says small-town values. This is the new paradigm for CEOs.

We wholeheartedly agree with Ron, and that's why we like to see the term *health care* separated out into two words—health and care—so that it properly emphasizes the critical role those of us in the profession play in looking after those who need our help. Isn't that what you do when you live in a small town? And isn't any hospital community really like a small town, made up of all sorts of different people who know one another, see one another, and work with one another every day, for years on end? When you are able to consider someone else as a neighbor in a small town, you will find it easy to care about that person's well-being.

To that same point, consider the following story told to us by Melody Trimble, CEO of Sparks Health System:

> One time I was walking the halls of the hospital when I saw a man who looked rather tattered and torn. My heart went out to him, and I felt compelled to wish him a blessed day. The man then asked me to stop. While I admit to being a little scared at first, I walked up to him with a smile. He said, "You know, I was going to kill myself today. I was just hoping someone would be nice to me."

This real story from a real person confirms the power of true kindness. As the saying goes, "Hey, you never know . . ." We never know how we impact the lives of those with whom we work and live. And that is the sort of caring we need to make sure our employees sense from us—because that sort of caring reminds them that they, too, must be caring in their jobs. Because none of us ever know what kind of impact we may have, at any moment, on the patient experience.

GIVE PERMISSION TO CARE

So, back to the question at hand: Can you teach someone to care? The answer, we feel, is that most people do intuitively care already—they just need to be shown that it's okay to show it. Not only that, but also that they will be rewarded for demonstrating how much they care. And you don't have to be a clinician to show that you care. You can be, for example, an executive, a cook in the cafeteria, or a janitor.

The solution, just as we discussed in the last chapter, is for leaders to step in and open the door for everyone to act, in large and small ways, on those innate caring feelings. We need only to lead by example and to give our people permission to care. That's why you can find a hospital president wandering the halls of a three-million-square-foot hospital from midnight to 3:00 a.m., delivering cookies and connecting with staff members. Taking the time to show that you care requires purpose and action—you can't fake it. When you do take the time to demonstrate that you care, however, appreciation, respect, and a sense of camaraderie soon follow. From there, it becomes a self-fulfilling and virtuous cycle; those caring feelings go viral.

Consider the following tale shared by Jim Hinton, CEO of Presbyterian Healthcare Services in New Mexico:

> There's a story that I tell at our new employee orientation
> sessions every other week, and it has to do with a nurse who
> was caring for a patient in our cardiac area. The patient's

family flew in on short notice from a rural part of New Mexico. They didn't have a chance to pack any clothes. And so, after a couple of days, the nurse noticed that the family members were wearing the same clothes. So she walked in one day with a stack of scrubs and asked if the family would like to change into the scrubs so she could take their clothes home overnight, wash them, and bring them back in the next day. I tell that story because, to me, it exemplifies the kind of backflips that our employees will do to help a family or a patient in need.

When you see a coworker with that kind of dedication to caring for patients, it is almost contagious.

Now, it's important to acknowledge that not everyone shows how much he or she cares in the same way, and the two of us are perfect examples of this. Britt, for instance, is a big hugger—he isn't afraid to lay a bear hug on just about anyone. In that way, he is able to break down physical barriers between people, which means that many of his employees return the favor by planning sneak-attack hugs on him whenever they can catch him off guard. Britt attributes his own managerial style to the weeks he spent in a hospital as a fifteen-year-old after a fire burned some 20 percent of his body. While the pain was excruciating, Britt's most prevalent memory of that time is the love he received from the people taking care of him. While he wasn't born with a scientific mind (far from it!), he knew he had other talents—such as his naturally friendly personality—that he could use as a way to bring that same kind of love, kindness, and caring to people. And he did so, caring for people around the world first as an LDS church missionary and more recently as a hospital CEO.

Paul, if you recall, is far more introverted than Britt. He's just not as comfortable going up to people and giving them a good squeeze, or even stopping to chat about their weekend and ask how their kid's Little League game went. He's just not wired that way. And that's totally okay, because he finds other ways to demonstrate the values he learned from his parents—namely, the Golden Rule of treating others the way you'd like to be treated.

For example, Paul has come to rely on a system that reinforces the sense of caring at the very core of his company: a program he helped create, called Beryl Cares. The Beryl Cares committee manages a website and database that keeps track of everything from important dates (birthdays, anniversaries, and such) to any news relevant to each employee, such as any deaths or sicknesses in the family or even a recent accomplishment (finishing a marathon, for instance). When an important event or date occurs, the system sends Paul and the other company leaders an e-mail with the information along with a picture of the person involved. Despite living in our age of instant electronic communication, Paul spends fifteen minutes every morning putting together handwritten notes on Beryl Cares stationery for a variety of celebrations, condolences, and events that are important to the members of his "family." He sends the notes to the employees' homes. While writing the note doesn't take a substantial amount of time, it's a moment that he can dedicate to a BerylHealth family member when that person might need it most.

But the caring culture of BerylHealth extends beyond Paul's relationship with his employees; it connects each and every coworker. That's how, for instance, everyone at BerylHealth was able to rally to the cause of two patient experience advocates, twin twenty-year-old brothers, whose apartment burned to the ground with all their belongings in it. With the help of the Beryl Cares committee, folks rapidly rallied around the brothers—raising $1,500 (which the company matched), holding bake sales to raise additional funds, and even offering to donate vacation time to help the two young men get back on their feet.

It is truly powerful to see how much people care about one another and how quickly they will unite and even sacrifice to do things for one another. Andy Leeka of Good Samaritan Hospital explained how it works—kind of a tit-for-tat, you watch my back and I'll watch yours situation—by sharing a story about Maria, an environmental services worker who brings in homemade tamales for Andy and the other associates from time to time:

> I know Maria. I know her family. I know about the tragic death of her son and attended his funeral. When her $400 was stolen that she was going to use to purchase groceries, I handed her $400 from my wallet to replace it because I am going to take care of her. I am going to take care of Maria, and Maria is going to take care of me. Maria is going to take care of the patients, the lobby of the hospital, and enthusiastically take on duties not even assigned to her. Maria is not going to allow a patient, visitor, employee, or volunteer to slip and fall if something spills on the floor. And Maria

is not going to walk by trash in a hallway or allow areas or our hospital to become dirty. Maria and I are committed to a safe and clean hospital. I am committed to Maria.

As Andy points out, people who work closely together benefit when they care about one another's well-being. Sometimes people will even step up all on their own to take care of one another. A great story along those lines almost happened by accident: A few years ago, Paul's lease on a company car (a 2000 Toyota Camry) was about to expire. But Paul decided that rather than turn it back in, the company would donate the car to a lucky employee—someone chosen by his or her peers. Now, the cynic in you is thinking that just about everyone would have put his or her own name in the hat and lobbied colleagues to help him or her land a gently used car. But when we tallied the votes to name the winner, there was one name (let's call him "Michael") who collected far and away the most votes. Unbeknownst to Paul and the other BerylHealth leaders, Michael didn't have a car—he had given his to his mother, whose own car had recently broken down. Michael had been forced to walk seven miles to get to work every day—and another seven to get home!—all under the blazing Texas sun. We all thought he'd been looking trim (in fact, he had lost forty pounds in just a few weeks), and now we knew why. More important, his peers knew the answer to his problem, and they stepped up to deliver a grand and heartfelt gesture.

Do you think being recognized by the team made an impact on Michael and the kind of engagement he felt toward the company and his coworkers after that? This is the kind of thing that can happen, regardless of the field you work in, when you give people the freedom and the opportunities to show how much they do care about one another. But in the health care field, where patients are in crisis and employees face trauma and tension every day, it can mean the difference between simply doing the job and truly loving the job.

RECOGNIZE AND REWARD CARING

If we want to encourage this above-and-beyond level of caring in our people—and we should want exactly that, both for the success of the company and for the best possible patient experience—it's absolutely critical to find ways to reward employees for their outstanding work. By recognizing the care that goes into each employee's performance, we can demonstrate that we have noticed the employee and that we care about him or her.

What's interesting, though, is that the rewards people really want, contrary to popular opinion, are rarely financial. In fact, the rewards many people value the most are those that they don't even collect for themselves. At Medical City, for example, there was a first-generation U.S. citizen named Bob who helped start a program called Our Children Matter. Bob and his partners in this effort devised a program where employees could essentially reward the accomplishments of their children. Kids who earned straight As, were accepted into a prestigious college, or achieved Eagle Scout rank got to come into the hospital and, in front of a big crowd, receive what looked like an Olympic gold medal.

And as much as the kids up on stage beamed, it was their folks who really shone in the wake of the recognition their kids were receiving from their other "family members"— their fellow employees. It was a beautiful thing to see.

It's important to note that this was the sort of program that could have been taken over by the hospital—as executives, we could have stepped in and taken control of it or co-branded it in some way. But we quickly realized that the greatest thing the leadership group could do was actually to step aside and remove any obstacles to making the program as organic as it needed to be. We let the hospital employees run the program for their colleagues—that was how we showed we cared about what was important to the employees. It was their "baby," and hijacking it would have taken away some of the beauty of the program.

Another example of ingenuity in recognizing the realities and concerns faced by our people comes from BerylHealth— in particular, the "Ask Paul" link on the company website. Through this link, employees can post anonymous questions to Paul and the leadership team. The idea, of course, was to give employees the chance to air their biggest complaints or get answers to their most pressing questions—to allow them to discuss things they might not be willing to ask in person. But you know what? Rather than pepper the senior leaders with questions about the strategic direction of the company, the bulk of the submissions centered on topics like "When is the toaster in the break room going to be replaced?"

The point here is that what's most important to you may be vastly different from what your employees are thinking about. That's why, when we wanted to start promoting an increase in BerylHealth's tuition reimbursement program (for high-performing employees who wanted to gain further education), we eventually shifted gears and created an annual scholarship program for children of employees. It is difficult to describe the emotions that parents experience when their employer helps fund their child's education and invest in their future. We quickly found out that connecting to an employee and his or her family via contributing to a college education can have a profound effect on how that employee views his or her job. When your people have that kind of encounter with the company, it's easy to imagine how they will answer the question "Does my employer really care?"

(NOT JUST) TALKING THE TALK

As we said earlier, to show that you really do care, you can't just talk the talk—you have to walk the walk. That's why, for instance, you could find Britt driving from the hospital in his 4x4 Jeep to the regional train station at 5:30 a.m. to pick up a group of nurses stranded by a nasty winter ice storm. No, he didn't do it just to make sure they got to work like they were supposed to. He did it because they wanted to get to work to help patients rather than be stuck inside a freezing-cold train station all day.

During that same ice storm, you could find Paul and his senior leaders manning the phone banks at Beryl-Health, knowing that many of the company's regular advocates were forced to stay home with children whose school days had been canceled. Rather than hiding out or becoming invisible on what could be a difficult and chaotic day,

Paul and his team stepped up to show that they were there for their people, that they understood family comes first. Think of the last time you actually had a boss cover for you at work, especially without laying a guilt trip on you. Come to think of it—has this ever happened to you? And more to the point, have you ever done something like this for any of your people?

Of course, on the path to showing that you care, you can also find yourself making missteps along the way. Britt, for instance, once wanted to take some time off-site with his chief nursing officer, to really listen and show that he cared what she thought. He hoped they could take some time to reconnect. But life in a hospital is busy, and you rarely have a moment for lunch, let alone getting off campus. So he never thought twice about taking her to his favorite restaurant—which happened to be Wendy's. Yes, that Wendy's. Now, as far as fast-food restaurants go, Wendy's ranks near the top. It's fast, and who doesn't love a delicious Frosty? Unfortunately, it never occurred to Britt that his CNO might be taken aback by his choice, that she might figure he didn't want to splurge on a nice lunch. Fortunately for Britt, his CNO eventually got the full story. And now, whenever Britt suggests they go out for a bite to eat, the CNO always insists on going to Wendy's, because she came to understand why he chose it in the first place. For him, it wasn't about the venue; it was all about the time and relationship. So when you demonstrate that you care about employees, it is necessary to explain your actions and understand how those actions will be received.

You and your organization must truly walk the walk

when it comes to caring. We can't stress enough how important this is! You need to keep challenging yourself to do things that are unique and special. As soon as your employees begin to see through a charade of meaningless gestures—to grasp that, in fact, you don't really, truly care—everything will come crumbling down around you. As Mike Packnett, CEO of Parkview Health in Fort Wayne, Indiana, told us:

> Without employee engagement, you're never going to get the kind of ultimate patient experience you're hoping for. You'll get something that is rather robotic instead. This is something I see and hear firsthand when I make rounds and hear how our new associates speak. But I think once we connect, once we can get any of our coworkers and physicians to connect their hearts with their heads on the idea that they all have such a huge part to play in the patient experience—once they get that, whether it be a housekeeper, a nurse, or a neurosurgeon, we're all in it to have absolutely the best outcome for that patient and his or her family—they realize it's all about the patient. They understand that this isn't just about a patient satisfaction score or an employee engagement score. That's the way we keep score, but it's not about the score—it's really about how it's reflecting what our own patients are telling us.

No doubt you have been a part of company celebrations or birthday parties taken straight from the script of the movie *Office Space*, where you can't find a smile anywhere and everyone present seems to be on autopilot. In those cases, employees simply don't trust that their employer cares—they sense that the boss is just "talking the talk." Rather than building up a sense of caring, these employers are in fact allowing it to erode. That's why Dr. David Feinberg, CEO of UCLA Health System, goes above and beyond to make real connections with his people. Every week, he invites random staff members to lunch, so they can share a meal as they share their opinions on their work environment and anything that will improve UCLA's care of employees, patients, and families. It is part of a broad effort, his desire to meet each of the company's seven thousand employees. "I am on a quest, ten people at a time," he told us. "And while I may not be able to name all our staff members"—we have to wonder, who could?—"I am fully committed to spending time with each person."

BerylHealth, too, tries to go beyond the normal in caring for its employees, by sending them handwritten postcards, not just on the anniversary of their employment at the company, but also to congratulate them on their son graduating college or their daughter winning the state softball championship. When people get these notes, they recognize that Paul and the company care about them. They say to themselves, "Wow, how did the boss know about that?" When you can make the connection between you and your employee about something personal—when you make it your business to know about what's important to them—the result is powerful.

Another case study in why caring matters comes from a hospital where an aspiring executive—let's call him "Larry"—thought the most effective way to achieve success was to "beat up" on his team so they would do what he thought they should do. Now, that isn't quite how he would have put it. No, instead he used plenty of corporate-speak like "We need to pick the low-hanging fruit" and "We need to stay focused and execute." Some days it sounded as though he were reading from *The Big Book of Corporate Clichés*. Most disappointing of all was the fact that Larry was a really, really good guy. He had entered health care with a purpose, but somewhere along the way he got fooled into thinking that it was all about him.

It all culminated when, one day, Larry took it upon himself to gather his team of fifteen or so direct reports and share with them his personal goals for the organization. The point, he said, was to get each and every one of them to help him fulfill those goals. Now, by this point in the chapter, warning bells and flashing lights should be going off in your head, to the tune of Larry, what are you thinking? And you're right: Larry's mistake was in thinking that the people working for him gave a darn about his goals, especially when he didn't seem to care a lick about theirs. Little did Larry know at the time, but he was about to go through a "learning moment."

Fortunately for Larry, he had a boss who saw potential in him. That boss pulled him aside and told him the cold, hard facts: that Larry needed to begin caring about his employees before they would begin caring about him. That's when the light bulb went on in Larry's head and his dramatic transformation began. The more Larry began showing his employees respect and paying attention to their careers, the more they rallied around the goals of the organization. By learning to care about his team members, Larry actually strengthened both the organization and his own credentials as a leader.

The lesson, of course, is this: If you as a leader want to improve your organization and achieve personal and professional satisfaction by moving down this road of caring, your efforts have to be purposeful and meaningful—they must be genuine and come from the heart. And you can't develop goals that serve some selfish, egocentric purpose— they must be for the greater good.

WALKING THE WALK

Genuine, purposeful caring—you almost have to drive it into your brain to make a constant effort to care for your people before the organizational culture as a whole becomes steeped in it. Sure, you're going to stub your toe every now and again by forgetting to send a card or celebrate an anniversary. But as long as it wasn't intentional, and as long as you've built up a strong track record of success, you'll find your employees to be forgiving. Still, you need to understand the risks, because you won't get that many free passes.

While Larry saw the light about truly caring for his people, not everyone will be able to cast aside his cynicism—which creates additional challenges for leaders. A story from Britt's early days growing up in Canada helps illustrate this. Many weekends, the Berrett family would load up their red canoe and head to the coast. Once there, they would arm themselves with "crab catchers"—poles with small baskets attached to the end—and then paddle about, looking for six-inch-long crabs, which they would scoop out of the water and into a bucket inside the canoe. The challenge was that the first crab would always start climbing out of the bucket, so you'd have to keep a close eye on him. But as soon as you added another crab or two, your problem was solved. Why? Because if one crab started trying to make his escape, clawing his way up the side of the bucket, the other crabs would grab hold and pull him back down.

The same thing exists within an organization. Oftentimes, people may try to take some initiative, to tackle something new and interesting, only to be dragged back down by the crabby cynics who aren't interested in trying anything new. They may wonder why you're trying to rock the boat—"Leave things as they are," they might say while turning a blind eye to the threat of the status quo and to the lost opportunities before them. The sad truth is, there will always be crabs ready to pull you and your coworkers down, which is why you need to develop the moral courage as a leader to break free from their grasp.

When you do take the time and make the effort to connect with your workforce in meaningful ways, the payoff is tremendous. Not only will your organization perform more effectively (which is nice), but also you will experience a personal ROI that you might never have expected (which can be even nicer). When you begin to reach out and learn more about the people you work with, you will find a sense of personal enrichment and camaraderie that goes beyond what any financial bonus could provide. You will also develop a deeper understanding of your colleagues, and we guarantee that you will be amazed at what you learn. When you begin to appreciate the depth of these people's lives—how they are building their families, taking care of kids and parents, fighting illness and other difficulties—it can be a humbling experience.

One such experience involved a BerylHealth employee—we'll call him "Brian." Brian was not only a great employee, but he was also a great person who, with his wife, had adopted two children from China as their own. One day, Brian, who was about fifty-five years old, received some shocking news: He had been diagnosed with stage IV cancer. It shook the company—everyone was upset by the news. But to his credit, when we held our holiday party a few weeks later, Brian insisted on attending even though he needed to be in a wheelchair to do it.

At the party, Paul made a big and unexpected announcement: Even though the company had failed to meet its financial goals for the year, he had decided to pay a partial bonus to each employee, because he thought it was the right thing to do. The resulting applause was, as you might expect, thunderous. But it was a letter Paul received a few days later that really blew him away. The handwritten letter was from Brian. After thanking Paul and asking about his health (Paul was recuperating from a pinched nerve in his neck at the time), Brian wondered if the bonus money announced at the party would be better spent elsewhere. "We're all thankful to have jobs here," Brian wrote. "And I'm not alone in thinking that perhaps you should reinvest it in growing the company." How many times have you heard of an employee who wanted to give back a bonus—let alone someone so ill, who could probably use the money himself?

Brian's story captures the theme of this chapter: that when you truly care about your employees, they will reciprocate those feelings both personally and in ways that actually improve the performance of the organization. You may not be able to find a line item that shows you how much caring matters, but your personal balance sheet will be much healthier as a result.

As we'll discuss in our next chapter, caring and having fun can also have an impact outside the walls of your organization.

CHAPTER FIVE

Outside the Four Walls

What if someone asked you, "What's at the center of your community?" Hmmm, interesting question, you might think. First off, you might wonder what this person means by community. After all, given the rapid changes in technology and social media, a community can involve just about anyone, anywhere. For our purposes, though, we'll focus on the notion of a community as the physical infrastructure of places where you live and work, and the people that live and work alongside you. That could be the greater metropolitan area of Dallas–Fort Worth, for instance, or perhaps just the streets that make up your suburban neighborhood.

Okay, with that out of the way, let's get back to the original question: What's at the center of your community? You could answer it in a very literal way—"Why, Main Street is the hub of my community, since it cuts straight through it"—or maybe in a more practical manner, as in, "My community revolves around my local Walmart, because I go there for everything." If you're not jaded politically, you might even have thought of an answer like "City Hall" or wherever you'd find the seat of your local government. Maybe you thought of your church or synagogue or a particular charitable organization. You probably didn't think of your local hospital or physician's office, though, because it's the kind of place that you don't think of until you need it. What's interesting is that whatever your answer was, it should tell you a lot about yourself and your priorities. It says even more if your answer involved the place you work.

Regardless of what you consider to be the center of your community, the more important notion is that all of us have interests and passions that exist outside of our workplace. And they often extend beyond our own personal interests like, say, woodworking down in the basement. Go to a soccer field on any given weekend, and you will see a mass of humanity: soccer players attacking the ball, kids screaming on the sidelines, cheering parents enjoying the festivities. And behind the scenes is an army of volunteers who so selflessly give of their time and energy to make it all happen. Many of these volunteers no longer even have children of an age to play the sport, but they have grown to love being part of something bigger. This is their community.

It all seems obvious, right? It's likely you already do engage in community-wide activities such as volunteering at local charitable events, coaching a youth sports team, or heck, even serving jury duty. You do these things because it feels like the right thing to do, or maybe because you just really like to do them.

But why should engagement with your community be limited to your life outside of work? What do you think begins to happen when you blur the lines between the organization you work for and the community surrounding it? What happens when you and your colleagues begin to think about having fun and sharing kindness not just with one another, but with the communities around you? Imagine the power when your organization embraces the team's interests and passions outside the four walls of work!

BEING PART OF A LARGER WHOLE

We are inspired by those who see a greater good and work to add something to that good, by those who invest in obvious acts of kindness and offer up subtle and seemingly effortless acts of caring. You can find many videos making the rounds these days via social media that show individuals touching the lives of others—even if it's just picking up a fallen book or randomly giving someone a handful of flowers. Sure, the advertising industry has captured the intrinsic goodness of these kinds of feelings for profit, but there is something else that goes beyond any commercial application, and it is pretty powerful.

Whether or not you realize it, the success of your company or organization—whether or not it operates within the health care sphere—isn't limited to the actions that take place and the people who operate within its walls (virtual or otherwise). In fact, you and your colleagues are all parts of a larger whole—a particular community or even multiple communities. Think about it: When you operate a hospital, your mission is to serve your community. But have you ever thought about what that really means, not just to yourself but also to your employees and colleagues? Did you ever think about how they might answer the question about the center of their community, and how that might drive what's most important to them? If your employees are active in coaching youth sports teams or organizing local food drives or taking part in cancer fundraising walks or whatever they are most passionate about, what do you think it means to them when their employer helps them in those efforts to give back to their community? In short, it could mean just about everything.

Here is an example: If you happen to be attending a swim meet or a soccer match in the Dallas–Fort Worth area, you will likely see dozens of ten-foot-by-ten-foot pop-up tents lining the sidelines. We need tents here in Texas to keep the heat off the spectators and give the kids a place to cool off. And how "cool" would it be for you, as a parent of one of the swimmers or players, to see a tent with your company's logo on it? What if there were dozens of tents with that logo? Wouldn't it give you a sense of personal pride, knowing that your employer was involved in your kid's sport and that your neighbors knew about it?

Well, this is exactly why Britt set aside a budget every year for his hospital to buy some five hundred such tents, which were made available to any employee willing to donate $50 to the hospital's hardship fund. While this is quite an investment made by the hospital—the tents cost about $100 each—the rewards are tremendous, because the employees themselves bring the organization's logo and values out into the community with them. That's when people begin to recognize that the hospital—the place where many of the community's members were born or where their loved ones were cared for—remains an essential member of the community even if we don't always think of it at the center.

Steve Rector, CEO of Regional Medical Center Bayonet Point, told us:

> We feel very strongly that as an organization, we should be an integral part of our community. The problem is, everyone has different ideas about how they want to contribute, so we had to adjust our thinking. We developed a program within our evaluation process so employees could participate in any community program they wanted to and get recognition for it. Our staff did everything from church-focused events to health screenings to coaching youth sports. We didn't care what it was—just be a part of the community!

Just as with the path to truly caring, it works only if you allow your people to rally around not what you think is important, but what's important to them.

What's the larger message here? Empowering your employees to engage with their community is also a tool for building greater engagement between you, your organization, and your employees—and, as you surely recognize by now (are we beating you over the head with it?), this will lead to greater experiences for patients and customers alike. To create this dynamic, though, as a leader you need to demonstrate the power and positive impact that results from serving others. As a boss or an employer, you must help facilitate that transaction, whether it involves handing out pop-up tents, organizing the cleanup of a local baseball diamond, or sponsoring a competitive dancing squad made up of your employees' children. As we emphasized in the last chapter, it's important to demonstrate caring and kindness to those you work with, so that they will do the same; likewise, it's essential to contribute to the hospital's community, as a way to give your employees and colleagues the "permission" to contribute to their community as well. Not only is it the right thing to do, but it will also drive your employee engagement levels through the roof.

Being part of a larger whole and working toward the greater good also happens to be a very personal issue for both of us—something that seems to have been hardwired into us at an early age. Forgive us for sharing a few stories here—they're not intended to be self-serving; they are to demonstrate the very personal way we each have learned to appreciate the importance of community in our lives. Perhaps these stories will help you realize how you can expand (or how you have expanded) your own sense of community—and that your experience of "community" doesn't need to end when you show up at the office.

For Britt, the importance of community struck home when he was nineteen and on a two-year mission to Peru with the LDS church. While visiting a hospital, he was deeply affected by the energy within the building—it was almost morgue-like, a place that people seemed to dread visiting. The staff ignored the two young missionaries and only pointed in the general direction of the church member whom they were there to visit. As the two young men departed, they were approached by numerous patients asking for help. They heard cries from adjoining rooms and felt compelled to stop and do whatever they could. And yet the staff just ignored those cries and even refused to lend a hand when the missionaries began to help the other patients.

The entire experience blew Britt's mind. Somehow, he realized, this hospital had removed itself from the greater community. How could a hospital, of all places, not seem to care about the people in its community? The role of a hospital, after all, is to use—in the best and most efficient way possible—the resources the community has entrusted it with. How could a hospital, then, not entwine itself within the community to accomplish that mission?

When he eventually returned home, Britt dedicated himself to teaching hospitals and health care organizations about how they can play an important role in blessing the lives of the people in the communities they were built to serve. Little did he know that his devotion to that idea would come full circle when, one Saturday morning, he felt the kind of excruciating pain that immediately made him think heart attack. After driving to the ER, where shocked workers first recognized him and then immediately began caring for him, Britt felt a sense of joy in knowing the kind of care he could expect from the place where he worked. It was an important moment and an inspiring experience that made him proud to be part of this community.

Paul's awakening to the power of community service occurred when he was in college. Growing up, he had always dreamed of being a doctor—something that pleased his mother immensely. But when he got a D in calculus his freshman year at UCLA, he knew his dream was over. That particular path wasn't for him—but that didn't stop him from reaching out in different ways, such as volunteering at the UCLA hospital's pediatric wing, which specialized in treating young kids with cancer. It was during his twice-weekly visits that Paul met José, an eighteen-year-old Mexican immigrant who spoke little English and was afflicted with a rare form of leukemia. Even with a language barrier to contend with (Paul's understanding of Spanish was limited to ordering from a menu), the two quickly bonded. So every week, Paul would wheel José in his wheelchair on long walks around the campus or over to the local Taco Bell to grab a bite to eat. It was during those walks that José got to show off his skills with the wheelchair—pulling wheelies and the like.

One day José asked Paul to push him to the top of a big hill and let him race down it. Figuring José was an ace with his chair, Paul agreed. You may not be surprised to learn that a near disaster ensued when the wheelchair quickly upturned, sending José flying. Fortunately, despite a few bumps and bruises, José got up laughing—which helped Paul deal with the guilt of nearly injuring his friend.

A few months later, José passed away. Soon after, when Paul ran into José's mom at the hospital, he told her how much José's friendship had meant to him. José's mom began tearing up as she told Paul how often José had spoken of him—he had even told her about the wheelchair incident. She thanked Paul for making a difference in her son's life—and her words were an act of kindness that has stuck with him ever since. The experience helped him understand the true meaning of being part of a community.

CREATING THE OPPORTUNITY TO SERVE

Perhaps you have memories of your own that have stuck with you, reminded you of the importance of community and giving back. The challenge, though, is that some of us might be more hardwired to serve than others—and some of us might not have had the chance to visit Peru or to meet someone like José. Not everyone has had an encounter that shapes their view of what giving back to the community can mean. Many people grow up without having any exposure to performing community service, thus they miss out on the tremendous sense of pride one gets from serving others. That's where you as a leader can help teach, encourage, and empower your people to act in a way that is true to their heart and spirit. For those of us who have learned to appreciate the joy of giving in this way, the rewards are seemingly endless.

If you aren't sure where to start or how to get your efforts off the ground, there are resources you can turn to for help. Just take a look around you, and you'll notice many different types of charitable programs looking for help in your own community—surely there's one that suits your organization and the type of service your people would like to provide. There are even groups that offer to help you find a way to serve. For example, an organization called Entrepreneurs for North Texas exists specifically to help companies that feel overwhelmed by the idea of offering organized community service for their employees. One event shepherded by this organization is Freedom Day; on each anniversary of 9/11, some four hundred volunteers representing twenty companies in the Dallas area show up at firehouses to help clean and repaint them, as a thank-you to those public servants who lost their lives on that tragic day.

At a recent Freedom Day, some seventy BerylHealth employees attended—which made a huge difference in the work that got done. Believe us, there's nothing easy about the assignment at these area firehouses—you can bank on working your butt off from 8:00 a.m. to 4:00 p.m. Plus, it was an investment on the part of the company because that Freedom Day took place on a workday. BerylHealth gets paid according to the minutes logged on the phone by its advocates, so the company was literally making an investment in the event. But consider how those Beryl-Health employees who were participating felt. Perhaps they were thinking, Wow, my company is willing to give up some revenue to help reach out into the community. They are actually paying me to help.

Many leaders are hesitant and fearful about these kinds of efforts because it's not something you can plot on a matrix—it's tough to quantify the rewards. But when you allocate resources and give your employees the freedom to use them within the community in ways they know will make a difference, amazing things result. Do you see how this kind of mind-set drives employee engagement?

Freedom Day is just one community outreach program in which BerylHealth employees participate. In fact, we created a committee called the Better Beryl Bureau, or BBB, that decides where the company spends its money and time in helping the community. What makes this approach powerful is that the passion comes from the employees, not just (as you see so often in other companies) from the top, with Paul telling everyone what they should participate in or to whom they should give back.

Similarly, in the ten years that Britt was at Medical City, the associates at the hospital would choose one major charitable effort each year as their focus for raising funds and volunteering. This list included the North Texas Food Bank, March of Dimes, and Habitat for Humanity. In total, the hospital contributed more than $1 million to those organizations over the course of a decade; by any measure, this made a huge difference in the lives of the hospital's community members. Again, the idea was that the leadership group would set the example and create an environment where employees feel empowered to act in what they see as the interests of their community. Standing shoulder to shoulder with all the other members of the staff, not just your immediate colleagues, as you worked toward a common charitable goal created an indescribable sense of unity. Collecting food items or carrying a stack of lumber to help a family in need reconfirmed to everyone that we are all in this together. As Bianca Jackson, the former head of Medical City's community awareness group (who now is director of fund development for Genesis Women's Shelter in Dallas), put it to us, "I firmly believe that the success of our community project has been because the executive team made it a priority and allowed us to embed it into our culture."

To put it another way, when you give your employees the opportunity to pick when and how they give back to the community, you align their emotional incentive to serve. Set the example as a leader, and then let your people follow—but in their own footsteps. Just wait until you see how they lock arms and tackle the project ardently together. The result is an unmistakable difference in the community—and a tangible difference in the culture of your organization.

THE CIRCLE OF GIVING

Of course, it's not always easy to get everyone to see the kind of payoff on the investment in time and money that giving back requires. At Medical City, for instance, Britt had budgeted $100 for each and every employee to use toward a community-driven initiative. All that was required in return was for the person to fill out a request detailing what he or she planned to do with the money. When Britt's CFO learned of the plan, though, he freaked out (to put it mildly). When he added up all those $100 grants and realized how much Britt intended to commit, he saw only one big hole in the budget rather than the potential payoff that would come from such an investment.

First off, not every employee has a cause he or she is passionate about. Those who did, though, were motivated to make a positive change—like the ten employees who pooled their money to sponsor their kids' dance team with $1,000. Now, from the CFO's perspective, this might have seemed like a waste of money. But what he overlooked was the investment an organization makes when it plows a ton of resources into marketing and advertising, buying billboard space and magazine advertisements in hopes of getting a return on that investment. Well, what happens when you hand just a fraction of that money to your employees, who then use that money to create a personalized, informal "marketing campaign"? Not only are those employees getting the hospital's name out into the community, but they are also showing through their smiles and sense of pride that they actually enjoy working for the organization—creating a positive image that automatically generates new leads in terms of both customers and employees.

Promoting and sponsoring employee-driven service pushes the organization out into the community, and more than that, it also brings the community inside the walls of the company. But don't let the free advertising be your motivational factor—that's just an unanticipated by-product. The true ROI is something you can't measure. Embracing the community as a whole means something special. It confirms what we already know: that investing in the community is a good thing that blesses lives. Dane Peterson, CEO of Emory University Hospital Midtown, reinforces this:

> One of our goals in improving employee engagement is fostering the ability of engaged employees to bless the lives of their families and their extramural organizations by being better leaders and followers outside of work. We feel that improving employee engagement is a way to build better communities.

The result of engaging your employees in service is that the community rallies around your organization and what you want to support. That's how you spread goodwill. A focus on the community also offers the bonus benefit of serving to break down barriers within your own organization, as members from different departments work hand in hand.

Organizing these kinds of community-driven programs are truly a win-win-win: for the individual, who wins by feeling good about giving back; for the company, which sees higher employee engagement; and, of course, for the community itself, which reaps the benefits of its engaged citizens.

GETTING YOUR HANDS DIRTY

We need to circle back and reemphasize one point: The larger the organization you run, the more difficult it can be to get everyone to understand the connection between employee engagement and community service. At Medical City, for instance, the employees periodically contributed to the "hardship fund," a pool of money used to help people in emergencies such as the sudden death of a loved one or their house burning down. But the hospital is part of a larger corporation, and here's the rub: At some point, one of the bean counters up the line found out about the money stashed away in the hardship fund, and Medical City was requested to donate those funds to the corporation's larger contribution effort to help support victims of a terrible disaster that was in the public eye at that time, Hurricane Katrina. Now, helping those whose lives were devastated by a hurricane is, no doubt, a noble cause. But even in such important efforts, when help is needed and given on a national scale, there is something missing. It is harder to connect with this sort of service, because the triggering event did not happen locally, and the results of your donation or service are not visible. The employees cannot personally connect with the cause, however worthy it is.

When it comes to the notion of community service, that's where the rubber meets the road in driving true engagement and commitment. Just checking a box and giving away money is simply not enough to effect change in the community or in your organization. You really have to show a commitment to the effort by getting in there and getting your hands dirty, so to speak, which is really what we're advocating. Taking visible action, not the amount of money involved, is the secret ingredient in the recipe for driving employee engagement.

There is an important footnote to the subject of serving your community: You shouldn't overlook taking care of your internal community as well. This gets back to the theme of our prior chapter on caring for those whom we work with. It's sort of foolish to ask your employees and colleagues to go out and give to the community if they are suffering themselves. Sometimes, helping the community begins with helping one another first. That means before we organize an outing to support a soup kitchen, we should be checking internally to make sure our own folks have everything they need. That's why at BerylHealth, for example, there is a directory of both internal resources and external community resources that employees can refer to when they, too, need help. The point is, while serving the community is vital for the health of your organization, you also can't forget who you are trying to serve in the process: your own people.

Remember, the way we define community might continue to change as well—it's a concept that is well chronicled in Robert Putnam's book *Bowling Alone: The Collapse and Revival of American Community*. Putnam describes a shifting of communities in recent years as individuals are changing how they interact with one another. Whereas people used to sit on their porches and chat with their neighbors, today they sit inside their homes as they chat on IM and share pictures on Facebook. Social media has opened up how we interact with one another in ways we never imagined—which has also created different definitions of what the term *community* means, especially across generations. Everyone sees the world differently, and that's okay. We can't be fearful of change. Rather, we need to embrace it, to accept that if our goal is to engage our employees, we need to be willing to view the world (and the idea of community) from their perspective. Taking a new approach can even help you identify whom or what cause you and your organization might choose to serve.

So ask yourself: What's at the center of your community? And don't forget to ask your employees, too. Soon you'll discover that identifying, creating, and serving your community are sometimes one and the same.

Unfortunately, in answering this question, you might also identify people who don't want to serve, don't want to get involved, don't want to become engaged with their work! Despite our faith in the power of engagement, we don't view this as a sort of heresy. It's just plain fact: Not everyone is going to be a good fit within your organization. If, after your good-faith effort, some of your people don't seem to get all the messages we've discussed so far, sometimes you have to learn to say good-bye—and that is the topic for our next chapter.

CHAPTER SIX

No Whiners, Losers, or Jerks

Let's not mince words: Mean people suck. With all due credit to the entrepreneurs who thought to put that slogan on a bumper sticker, the truth is that most of us already knew it was true because we've experienced it firsthand. We've learned to shy away from those folks around us who, like vampires, tend to suck the life, the fun, and the energy out of every situation. You know the kind of people we're talking about: whiners, losers, and jerks.

When you come across one of these energy drainers, you can't get away fast enough, and even when you do, it leaves an awful taste in your mouth. Like when you run into someone we might call a whiner in the break room: Someone who, no matter what, has something negative to say. Heck, the company might have just announced a company-wide bonus, and this person would find some way to turn it into a negative. "You can bet the executives probably paid themselves more than they deserved," the whiner might say.

A loser, on the other hand, is the person who pops up when you're late getting into work because you blew a tire on the freeway, the person who feels compelled to chime in and tell you how much worse he or she had it. "Oh, well I had four flat tires and a blown gasket," the loser says, while you sigh and wonder what a gasket is anyway.

As bad as whiners and losers are, jerks may in fact be the worst of all. These people are toxic and corrosive—a negative influence on others. To give you an idea of the kind of person we're talking about, consider an experience Britt had a few years ago. As head of Medical City, he received e-mail all the time from the nursing staff, about everything from shift duties to changes in benefits. After one such change in the benefits plan, Britt received a flurry of e-mail from the staff. The tone of most of this e-mail was, as you would expect, fairly formal and respectful. But one nurse—let's call her "Nurse Ratched"—was, to put it plainly, just rude. Taken aback by the note, Britt, who didn't know Nurse Ratched particularly well, thought that she must have been having a bad day, so he gave her a pass and simply wrote back, asking for some clarification of the point she had raised.

Wouldn't you know it? Britt got a response from her that was even snarkier than the first. Now, Britt may be a bit old-fashioned, but even workers of a younger generation should know better than to flat-out insult the CEO of their hospital. A bit peeved at this point, Britt took the initiative to have a chat with the chief nursing officer to find out what was going on with Nurse Ratched that might explain her rude behavior.

You won't be surprised to hear Britt quickly found out that the CNO had been having problems with this nurse from the day she was hired. Not only was she disrespectful to her colleagues, she was downright mean and condescending to patients. "So why haven't you fired her?" Britt asked his CNO. "Do you have the paperwork to back up her problems?" The CNO explained that she did have the paperwork, but she was short-staffed as it was, and this nurse covered a particularly busy shift.

It can be difficult to fire an employee, even if you have good reason. There is always a way to rationalize or find an excuse about why you should keep someone. But, as Britt explained to the CNO, if you had a loved one who needed care at the hospital, would you want this nurse attending to him or her? Of course not.

After that meeting, Britt invited Nurse Ratched for a visit in his office along with a representative from the human resources department. Doing his best to put a positive spin on the situation, Britt explained some of his concerns about Nurse Ratched's behavior. Rather than an apology or even an explanation, he only got more grief in return. Seeing the situation for what it was, he stood up, walked around his desk, and (as politely as he could) told Nurse Ratched that he was firing her immediately due to her excessively negative behavior. Nurse Ratched went as pale as a ghost and quickly tried to backpedal with a stream of apologies. But it was too little, too late. The only thing left to say was "Good-bye, Nurse Ratched."

You wouldn't believe the reaction of everyone at the hospital when they learned that Nurse Ratched had been let go. The news spread like wildfire, and it was almost like the feeling you got as a kid on the last day of school. People seemed to be physically relieved to see her go. One employee even suggested we throw a party to celebrate her departure. We can only imagine what her patients felt. This story goes to show you that whiners, losers, and jerks are not just problematic in and of themselves—they can actually create a ripple effect of negative energy that, in the end, creates bad experiences for their colleagues and, in turn, patients and customers. As Tom Royer, past CEO of CHRISTUS Health in Irving, Texas, told us:

> Where we are successful, we have the right people [working for us]. Where we are not successful, we have the wrong people. If we are 99 percent correct in what we do, and you are the one patient who is the other 1 percent, that's not good. The biggest barrier is the tolerance of mediocrity [in our people]. There's nothing worse than good people becoming mediocre.
>
> When people are comfortable in their mediocrity— when they put in little effort at work and simply plod along, day after day—there is still hope to turn them around and remind them that working in health care is a calling.

But whiners, losers, and jerks are worse than just mediocre; they have a negative effect on the workplace. They don't buy into the idea of becoming engaged with their work, and they probably never will. Find them now, and weed them out as soon as possible.

FIND THE RIGHT FIT

Let's be honest: All of us at one time or another have been prone to tasting a morsel or two of gossip, which is often dished out in a very negative manner. What we don't realize is that we are actually feeding those folks who serve up that negative gossip; they thrive when they have an audience for their vitriol. These people are hardwired to whine and complain and draw undue attention to themselves. With mean people, it's all about me, me, me. This brings up an interesting parallel for those of us who work in health care: Can you see the similarities between this kind of behavior and an infectious disease? Meanness is a toxic behavior, and it tends to spread quickly. So what might you do to combat such an illness? Why, you'd eradicate the source—by whatever means necessary.

At BerylHealth, for example, there was a call center manager who was brought on mostly due to her impressive work history at other organizations. Knowing that the BerylHealth team was growing, Paul and the other senior leaders thought her experience working in bigger call centers would help them scale faster and more efficiently. Boy, were they wrong. Unfortunately, it took them a while to figure it out. You see, the woman—let's call her "Sally"—knew how to interact with the senior leaders and was always e-mailing metrics and statistical information to show that she was on top of things. But back among her team, she was a command-and-control leader of the worst kind, and she made the experience of those working with her a sheer misery.

It soon became clear to Sally's peers in other departments that something was wrong. It wasn't until the employees took a stand and approached senior management about Sally a year later, though, that the gears were put into motion to get her out of there. In this case, Ber-ylHealth got lucky when its employees stepped up to the plate to help the organization expunge a cancer rather than simply getting sick of it and leaving—something that happens all too often in organizations. And losing great people because we as leaders are afraid or ignorant of the behaviors of those few bad apples is something an organization simply cannot afford—especially these days, when it is hard to find and keep great people. Once we have found superstars, we don't want to lose them.

Let's be clear: No one enjoys firing someone (at least, they shouldn't), especially in an economy like the one we've been suffering through, where there is little guarantee someone can land another gig. We also have to face the fact that Sally was our mistake: If we had done better work up front, we wouldn't have hired her and therefore would never have been forced to let her go. But regardless of whose fault it is, there are times when letting someone go is a necessary evil—when it benefits the whole of the organization. As Gary Newsome, CEO of Health Management Associates in Naples, Florida, put it, "High performers will disengage if we allow mediocrity to exist. 'B' players need to show signs of being an 'A,' and 'C' players should be moved out." For the good of the overall group, it's the only solution.

We're playing with live ammunition here, folks, and you don't have time to mess around. The longer you wait to make the decision, the more likely it becomes that the disease will spread. That means you have to act as quickly as possible when you know you have a problem child in the house. And that's what makes it hard sometimes, because you're not dealing with a department or something that's widespread. It's just one person. And if that person can't or won't make the necessary changes, he or she has to go.

That, of course, is when the excuses and the enabling come into play: We hate firing people, so we give malcontents extra attention and multiple chances, hoping to turn things around. We're here to tell you that this is a big mistake. By hemming and hawing, you're actually harming yourself and the organization as a whole. Everyone can see that you're coddling a problem person, a person no one likes to work with anyway. You need to make the move to get rid of the bad egg, pronto.

When you are an organization trying to implement a culture of engagement, to give everyone a fair shake you have to be willing to bring everyone together and tell it like it is. You may have to call an organization-wide meeting (as Paul has done at BerylHealth from time to time) where you state, in very clear and simple terms, that anyone who wants to work for the organization has to follow certain rules when it comes to his or her behavior toward one another. "We are on a mission," Paul will say. "If you don't believe in that mission, we would like you to leave. And if you refuse to leave, we will hunt you down and root you out." No more Mr. Nice Guy!

Tony Armada, CEO of Advocate Lutheran General Hospital, put it a little more gently:

> Those 10 to 15 percent of your employees who are totally disengaged are detrimental within your organization. We

spend too much time on those individuals instead of spending time with the solid performers.

The point is, you simply cannot allow any individual to hold your organization hostage or pose a threat to the kind of culture you are trying to build. Sometimes leadership means being willing to stand up and make the tough decisions, to demonstrate the moral courage to say good-bye to the whiners, losers, and jerks.

STAND UP TO THE BAD APPLES

Let's not overlook the kind of stakes involved in these decisions. Consider that the lifetime value of a single patient to a hospital is some $250,000. Well, what do you think happens when someone like Nurse Ratched treats that patient? In the wake of a poor patient experience, that patient will not be coming back the next time he or she gets sick, which means you just lost a valuable long-term customer—and probably the rest of the family, too.

It's humbling to think that a single individual could wreak such havoc with the future of your organization. But given the new realities of health care, where patients have more choice than ever before, as a leader you can't afford to ignore, overlook, or rationalize keeping your bad apples. The risks are simply too high.

Think about a story our friend, Dr. David Feinberg, CEO of UCLA Health System, told us about his dad, who, at age seventy-five, decided to get hip surgery. But rather than get the procedure done at his son's hospital, the elder Mr. Feinberg went to a rival facility, a place he had gone before. Although David had tried to get his dad to spend his recovery time at home, Mr. Feinberg refused to let David pay for it, so he stayed in the hospital instead. But it took just a single night before David's cell phone rang: It was his father, and based on the lousy experience he was having in recovery with the nurses, he wanted David to come help him get out of there. "I'll never come back here again!" Mr. Feinberg yelled into the phone. Translation: That hospital just lost a longtime customer.

Let's not forget the great power of choice that patients have over where they go to receive care and the providers from whom they receive it. Just a single bad apple among your staff could end up becoming a major financial liability for the organization.

And we don't mean to pick on just nurses. Physicians, more than ever, are being made accountable for their actions and attitudes toward not just patients but colleagues as well. We heard a story about a crew of nurses who found a way to stand up to a particularly abusive doctor by simply surrounding him and, even as he yelled at them, standing silent—a practice they called a "code white." As any good physician will admit, if a doctor's attitude becomes a threat to patients or coworkers—regardless of how skilled a physician he or she might be or how much revenue his or her services generate for the hospital—the hospital leadership has to stand up and make the decision to let that person go.

This same line of logic applies to anyone in the organization, even if he or she doesn't deal directly with patients. "I won't hold on to anyone who is a negative influence, no matter how much money he or she makes for the organization," Dr. Feinberg told us. Why? Think about the sort of daisy-chain effect a single bad encounter can have. What if, for example, a nurse is having problems with the printer at her station? But when she calls up the IT department, the guy she talks with is rude and disrespectful. (You can almost hear the first question: "Are you sure it's plugged in?" Bah.) Can you guess what happens next? Maybe the nurse then has to interact with a dietician on the floor, and because the nurse is so ticked off at the IT guy, she vents by letting the dietician have it, coming at her with both barrels. The dietician might then pass all this negative energy along to another colleague or, worse, directly to a patient. Do you see where we're going here? The negativity goes viral and becomes a threat to literally everyone.

You simply can't make excuses for whiners, losers, and jerks, regardless of what role they play in your organization. Mike Packnett, CEO of Parkview Health, would back us up on that:

> By our nature, as leaders in health care, we are rescuers. But we can't afford to rescue people anymore; if we do, we can't get to where we need to be. I think, over the last couple of years, we've done a lot better job of really understanding that we can't rescue everybody, that we can't transform everyone. I think we, as leaders, have to help those folks get to where their fit is.

What Mike is saying, quite diplomatically, is we have to let those folks go.

Unfortunately, many leaders begin to make excuses when it comes to firing an employee, principal among them that the HR department is somehow a nuisance or a barrier to getting things done. One executive Paul met at a conference, for instance, blamed his HR department for dragging its feet when it came to letting people go, forcing him to wait up to two years before he could fire someone. In his words, HR was "the enemy." We're here to inform you that if you believe this, you're missing out. The folks in HR aren't mere paper shufflers to be ignored and vilified. Instead, they should be among your closest allies. In fact, a vibrant HR department is a cornerstone of the future success of every organization.

When he started out at his hospital in Dallas, Britt found that the human resources department was located four buildings away from the main hospital, across a skybridge and hidden in an office building. Really? The most important resource is our team, and here we have a group of professionals banished to beyond the beyond? How can we expect to access their expertise and call upon their support as we navigate through various challenges when it comes to an organization's most important asset: our people? Britt relocated the entire human resources department to the main building, where it moved into a recently vacated patient care area. You can bet that move sent a huge message to the rest of the team about the importance of the human resources professionals.

Your HR department not only offers guidance when it comes to your team, but it ensures compliance with all sorts of regulations. When your HR people ask for documentation on an unsatisfactory employee, it's not that they want to become a barrier—they just want to protect the organization against any legal entanglements. Getting fired should never come as a surprise to anyone. Everyone has the right to know where they stand; before it comes to a dismissal, an employee's file should always have the proper documentation to support your position. The most challenging cases, though, involve an employee who is highly skilled in a technical area but has poor team and behavioral skills. As Steve Moreau, CEO of St. Joseph's Hospital of Orange, told us, "Those are the people who are harder to get rid of, because the team values their insights. But if you don't get rid of people who are disruptive and problematic for team performance, you'll destroy team culture."

Let's not overlook the fact that terminating someone's employment is a major life change for that person, on par with going through a divorce. You shouldn't take such decisions lightly—that's part of remaining true to your commitment to living as a caring organization. Having an HR partner who helps you approach that process with as much respect and compassion as possible can turn a difficult event into a positive experience for the organization as a whole.

That said, if your HR people have lost their sense of balance about what's most important—the organization, not their procedures—then you may have to consider changing them out as well. We know that sounds harsh, but it's the simple truth.

LEAN ON YOUR TEAM

We also need to rely on our HR team to be our first line of defense—an early-warning system of sorts—against the onslaught of whiners, losers, and jerks. That means asking the question, "How did a person like Nurse Ratched ever get in the front door in the first place?" We also need to be willing to ask, "What can we do to ensure it doesn't happen again?" That's not to imply that the responsibility for finding the right people is HR's alone. In fact, an effective leader has the critical function of rallying everyone on the team to this cause.

Knox Singleton, CEO of Inova Health System, told us:

> I think one of the light bulbs that's gone on for us is that we often hire a sow's ear, shall we say, and then try to develop the person into a silk purse. I think the high-performing service organizations have really shown that with a fair amount of front-end discrimination—not of the improper type, but of the proper, healthy type—you can actually identify and selectively hire folks who really have a personality and a heart for service.

If we as an organization can do a better job screening applicants for jobs, after all, we won't have to go through the distasteful process of letting someone go. That means working harder not just to, as the old saying goes, "put butts in seats," or even to find the most skilled candidates around. No, what we as an organization need to do is find the folks with the right skills who also fit the culture we're trying to build. All too often we become blinded by the big names and resumes loaded with experience, but we fail to dig deep enough to find out what a person is really like to work with. That's why Alan Channing, CEO of Sinai Health, starts the evaluation process—and the introduction to team culture—as early as the new employee orientation:

> We've thanked a few people even before orientation is over and said that it won't be a good fit. So we set the expectation and pattern early on. People comment on how friendly everyone is. I haven't asked people to do that. It is just what we've become. When you are working in a team that is sharing that kind of behavior, you either get with the program or you don't stick around.

Because ensuring a good fit is so important, Britt's organizations have traditionally shied away from hiring contract nurses. Nothing against the nurses themselves, as most are highly skilled and hardworking. But independent contractors don't have any skin in the game, so to speak, in terms of buying into the organizational culture. They won't be around for long, so why should they participate in the hardship fund or even the annual Christmas tree ornament exchange? Those partnerships tend to cost the organization more in the long run.

At BerylHealth, the goal is to bring someone on board as part of a lasting relationship, to welcome him or her as part of the family. Job applicants go through a rigorous series of interviews, in a variety of situations and locales both inside and outside the office, that allow the organization to get a better sense of the person and how he or she interacts with others and connects with the organization's mission, vision, and values. This interview process isn't just a top-down effort: Each candidate meets with people at all levels of the organization as a way to gauge how well he or she will mesh with the company culture.

To begin this evaluation, it can be useful to ask a candidate about his or her favorite and least favorite experiences with former employers; the answers can tell you a lot about the person's ability to be a caring coworker. Your HR department can provide a healthy list of evaluative tools that make for a more insightful look at the person you may be inviting to join your team. Personality tests are a really effective tool—an early-warning system of sorts—to help spot the rotten apples through the camouflage of an impressive resume. There are also numerous recruiting tools and assessments of clinical skills that might just add that important point of information you need in making a decision. Do yourself and the rest of your team a favor by taking a long look at the results of these tests. Nobody is perfect, so keep your expectations in check. But always remember that the cost of bringing on the wrong person is just too high a price to pay.

The same principle even applies to volunteers, those people willing to donate their time and energy to taking care of patients. "Wait a minute," you're probably saying. "Are you telling me you'd fire a volunteer? Are you sure you guys aren't the jerks here?" Well, we'll leave the jerk issue aside for a moment and focus on the first question by sharing a story. Back when Britt worked at Medical City, there was a brilliant director of volunteers named "Lindsey," whose job was to supervise some four hundred to five hundred volunteers—a small army, to be sure. Most of these men and women had received care at the facility or had seen their loved ones treated there, and these folks tend to wear their hearts on their sleeves when they show up, because they truly want to give back. But just as you find with employees, there are also volunteers who come in with a "me first" attitude. They are more interested in doing what they want to do rather than doing something that might actually be helpful.

In one case, an individual who showed up to volunteer had a mean streak and a sense of entitlement—perhaps fueled by the fact that her parents were major donors to the hospital. That created a sticky issue for Lindsey. She wanted this woman out, but could she risk severing the ties to important funders? To her credit, however, Lindsey made the wise and difficult decision to tell the volunteer that her services were no longer welcome at the facility. And, as we saw in the Nurse Ratched story, the other volunteers seemed to get an amazing boost from this turn of events because they, too, didn't enjoy working with this particular woman. We know it might sound a little extreme, but you need to put even volunteers through your screening process. Making sure they fit is essential to the organization's cultural health and harmony.

Let's be honest—every organization will have some number of disengaged employees. The key, as Dane Peterson, CEO of Emory University Hospital Midtown, told us, is to create a culture where the engaged employees significantly outnumber the disengaged, perhaps by a four-to-one or even a five-to-one ratio. "When this happens, the disengaged go quiet and lose their negative impact on the culture," he pointed out. That should be one of your goals as a leader: to reduce the impact of your disengaged employees so you can spend more time with the engaged ones.

SHIFT YOUR FOCUS

Let's pause for a moment. Look what we've gone and done by spilling a few thousand words sharing these negative stories. We've fallen into the same trap that so many organizations do when they allocate far too much time and energy tending to the whiners, losers, and jerks, rather than celebrating their star performers. Let's remember what we have said in a prior chapter about our belief that most people are, in fact, good people. That goes double for anyone working in the health care field—those people who possess huge hearts and a deep caring for their fellow man. Those are the people we want to support, cultivate, and work with. Dane Peterson had this to say in addition to his prior comments:

> My overall feeling about disengaged employees is that I try not to think about them or spend an inordinate amount of time with them. The job is too difficult to have the disengaged suck the life out of you. Instead, spend time with your engaged employees to find out what needs to be improved.

Case in point: The mother of two patients—twin boys who were born premature and being cared for in the hospital's neonatal intensive care unit—wrote to Britt in a personal e-mail:

Hi, Britt.

I want to share an incredible story about one of the nurses in the neonatal intensive care unit, Thao. I spoke to Thao on the phone last Tuesday and happened to mention that in two days, we would be celebrating our ten-year wedding anniversary by enjoying a meal out. When Jeff and I walked in the NICU doors that Thursday, the first thing Thao said was, "Happy anniversary!" We were shocked that she had remembered.

While we were there visiting, she asked us where we were going to dinner. Well, fast-forward a few hours to the end of our dinner. The waitress asked us if we wanted dessert, and we said, "No, thank you."

The waitress then said, "Well, Thao called and is buying you dessert for your anniversary." Thao had called the restaurant and described to the waitress what we were wearing so she could find us. I teared up at the table, and Jeff said it was the most touching thing anyone had ever done for us. When we called Thao on the way home to thank her, she said, "You guys have been through so much, you deserve to have a special night."

To which I replied, "Thao, you are taking care of our kids—we should be buying you dessert!"

I thought you would like to hear that story. What an amazing heart Thao has, and we are so blessed that she is taking care of our kids.

Stacey and Jeff, parents of Ben and William

Why do we spend so much time fretting and tending to Nurse Ratched when superstars like Thao—the ones who are enhancing the lives of our patients—get so little of our attention? By failing to acknowledge the efforts of those people who truly care, we risk losing them altogether because they'll begin to wonder what the organization's values truly are. And that can result in immeasurable costs to the organization.

Talented people want to work with other talented people. As we've discussed before, the majority of people in health care are kind and caring; they want to make a difference through their jobs. That's how you build high employee engagement scores and, as a result, great patient satisfaction results. So why aren't we spending more of our time encouraging and challenging the best rather than pandering to the worst? That's where you as a leader come in to set the example.

BerylHealth employs a program, for instance, that actively catalogs certain employees every three months as either high-potential or low-potential workers. If a person is singled out at one or the other end of the spectrum, he or she is then assigned a senior leader, a mentor of sorts. This mentor is available to help the individual identify next steps he or she can take to improve, which allows us to make the most of the high performers and give the low performers an opportunity to get on the right track.

Over the years, it's become apparent that the workers saddled with the "low potential" label often find themselves there mostly thanks to their attitude. It becomes the duty of their assigned leader to either coach them or, in a worst-case scenario, terminate them. The truth is, we've found, that negative people are often very difficult to turn around. So why keep investing our increasingly scarce time, energy, and resources in trying to do so? Why not spend those resources on the best of the best, since that's where we get the real return on investment: the patient experience payoff? It is critical for us, as leaders, to spend more time on making our stars shine even brighter by giving them new challenges and opportunities to grow.

It's regrettable that sometimes you'll lose good people. The era of lifetime employment at a single organization is long past, and people are more mobile than ever. Rather than fight this truism, embrace it. It merely emphasizes our point: that you need to open up the lines of communication, invest in your stars, and quit procrastinating about making the tough decisions you know you need to make about, as Jim Collins so aptly puts it in his best-selling business book *Good to Great*, "getting the right people on the bus." When the departure of good employees shakes things up at your organization, see it as an opportunity to bring in new blood and improve in an area you hadn't previously addressed.

More often, however, you'll find that the good people stay when the culture is right and they are a good fit; it's the "square pegs" who remove themselves from the "round hole." The more you emphasize your organization's core values—and make personnel decisions based on those values—the more you'll see people actually self-selecting themselves out of the organization. That can also mean sitting down with each of your employees and challenging them to put together a five- or ten-year personal vision, a written description about what they're doing in the future, as if they're already there. This can be a particularly useful exercise both for the individual and for you as a leader because you learn who sees themselves as a part of the organization for the long term.

In conducting this exercise with his employees, for instance, Paul learned that one of his executives saw himself running his own landscape business in five years. While that meant he would eventually lose this manager, Paul also knew he could help the employee develop the kinds of entrepreneurial skills on the job that would help him down the road while also helping BerylHealth in the short term. If, on the other hand, Paul had tried to clamp down on his manager's dreams, he could have ended up with a jerk on his hands.

"Hold on," you might be saying right now, "are you telling me that if I have a superstar working for me who wants to be some kind of landscaping da Vinci, and I don't support him, I'll be responsible for turning him into a jerk?" Well, not exactly. But consider what happens to people who don't have a dream, to people who lose hope. Perhaps your superstar will never become a landscape architect. But by being on his side and understanding some of his greatest hopes and aspirations, you become something more than a boss or an employer. All of us go through different phases in our lives—maybe this is just an idea, and your superstar will find that he is better suited to staying in the health care field and on your team. The real key is to know and love the members of your team, and to respect the commitment they make to that team—even if it's not forever.

But there are no guarantees in life. You might be the most tolerant employer ever, and encourage your employees to chase their dreams—but there's still no guarantee that your employees will open up and be honest about their future with the company. Consider the following story from Britt's past. One of the most dynamic areas of any hospital is the heart and vascular unit. We say "dynamic" because this area is both exciting and chaotic from a clinical standpoint, and because of that, the type of person the unit seems to attract is passionate and innovative. No kidding—there is something different about the men and women who are drawn to this field of work. Britt knows this from experience, and true to his personal values, he tried to be aware of the needs of the team members at Medical City. No losers: check. No whiners: check. No jerks: check. But in the midst of some critical changes within the unit—changes for the better, as everyone else cheered—one of the team's key leaders—let's call him "Steve"—submitted his resignation.

Steve left behind a team that was devastated by his surprise departure. This sudden resignation left Britt wondering how this could have happened. Just when he thought he was building teams and weeding out the dead wood in the name of the mission, vision, and values of the organization . . . Boom! He loses a superstar. Britt learned an important lesson that day: Everyone brings his or her previous life experiences to the game—a reality he uncovered by conducting some analysis after Steve's departure. It turns out that Steve had, at a prior place of employment, shared his desires and ambitions with his former boss—who then promptly punished him by reducing his responsibilities. So Steve's prior experience had taught him to keep his cards close to his chest and to reveal his career intentions only when it served his needs.

In any individual's work history these days, nothing is linear. A career doesn't move in a straightforward line from Point A to Point B then to Point C. Instead there is a basic migration from one position or accomplishment to the next, based on people's fundamental behaviors and foundational beliefs. That means even when we try to encourage our entire team to be open and transparent, sometimes even the superstars bring a little history along with them—for the good and for the not-so-good. So, you can't let one bad experience throw you off your mission. We know it's easy to fall prey to this trap. But as we say in Texas, "Cowboy up!" Let the surprises roll off your back, and take a step forward. Continue to focus on your mission, vision, and values as you build the right team—and don't forget to inspire, motivate, and encourage your star performers along the way.

There's no doubt this kind of thing takes work and commitment, but it's worth it. When employees feel confident that you have their best interests in mind, you can head off most surprises when it comes to good people leaving. Plus, it feels good to know you have contributed to someone's personal vision, even when it takes that person away from your organization.

If you as a leader have the courage to confront your less-than-worthy colleagues over the fact that they are truly square pegs trying to fit into a round hole, it can have a counterintuitive effect: You might actually see people with smiles on their faces after they've been let go. Maybe some of these whiners, losers, and jerks have become bitter about their job or position yet have been too afraid to make a change in their life, which results in a kind of resentful apathy. By confronting them with the truth, you might just set them free to chase the kinds of opportunities they truly mesh with.

Phew! The topic of this chapter was a tough one to discuss. We're glad you made it through. But we're not saying that making personnel changes is the only challenge facing executives of health care–oriented organizations—far from it! We're just saying that these internal issues should be addressed before moving on to the others. To learn more, turn the page and meet us in the next chapter.

CHAPTER SEVEN

Why Measure?

When you tell people you live in Texas, you tend to get a lot of different reactions. While neither of us was born here, it is our home now. So we get why people seem to either love it or leave it when it comes to the state. One thing you can't deny about Texans, though, is that they love their football. Texans are obsessed with football, and they show it by wearing team jerseys and caps just about wherever they go. And we're not just talking about professional teams like the Dallas Cowboys or the Houston Texans—people also proudly wear the insignias of college and even high school teams. If you don't believe us, check out the book *Friday Night Lights* by Buzz Bissinger (it was also made into a movie and a TV show if one of those is more your speed).

This whole notion of Texas football mania was brought home to Britt one Saturday when, on a shopping trip to his local Costco, he saw more than forty people standing around watching a Texas versus Oklahoma college game on the store's big-screen TVs, every one of them wearing jerseys and caps, and every one of them looking as if his entire life depended on the result of the next play.

Paul recalls when he noticed it too: When he first arrived in Texas, all his neighbors seemed to talk about was the result of the latest high school football game—even though none of them had kids in high school at the time! The simple fact is that people (especially Texans, apparently) are inspired by associating with winners. We tend to create a sense of identity that comes from being part of a winning team.

But while it's easy to know if your football team is winning, how do you know whether or not your organization is successful? "Why, that's easy," you're probably saying. "Winning in business comes down to whether you're profitable or not." While we won't disagree—after all, profits are the fuel that give you and your organization options for a path to future success—this is far from the only measure of a winning organization.

Blasphemy, you say? Not quite. Look, folks, your organization—like both of ours—is on a journey toward the summit of the mountain. The truth is, you might never reach the summit, but you are going to cross peaks and valleys on your journey toward it. And every time you crest one of those extraordinary peaks, you'd better make time to celebrate it as a way to mark the progress you've made across those dark valleys. Those peaks, when you take the time to notice them, are all the other metrics aside from financial performance—specifically, employee engagement and patient/customer satisfaction scores—and you need to be paying attention to them in order to beat the drum of progress. In fact, if you're focused on celebrating the engagement levels of your employees first, and the satisfaction of your patients and customers second, we can almost guarantee that you're going to see financial success.

Don't believe us? How about hearing it from Tony Armada, CEO of Advocate Lutheran General Hospital, who shared some advice a mentor once gave him: "If employees and physicians are happy, you'll get an increase in volume. If you increase volume, you'll find ways to decrease cost. With that, you'll increase margin and be able to invest back in employees." We couldn't have put it better ourselves.

Unfortunately, we've found that most health care organizations these days, unlike Tony's, have been looking at this equation "bass-ackward," where everything starts and ends with the financials. It makes for scary situations for today's leaders, especially in the health care realm, because they were taught to focus on the balance sheet alone—they have never received the kind of management and organizational training a leader really needs to be successful. It's a monumental problem we'd like to help solve.

FINANCIALS COME THIRD

It all comes down to this: Health care leaders need to focus more on the people, not the numbers. Allow us to explain.

When you look back at the history of health care, it all began with people wanting to nurture and care for those of us who were sick. But it wasn't a very scientific process— the first surgeons we had were also our barbers! We didn't even have what we would call a "hospital" until the 1800s, and even then the element of compassion was more evident than the study of science—there was a religious connection to hospitals, and the nurses were nuns. The focus in those times was on understanding what kinds of things were making people sick and how to make them get well—not on measuring how the caregivers were doing. That meant data was at best inconsistent, if it existed at all.

Compare that to today, where it seems all anybody can say is, "The numbers just don't add up," and "The health care system is broken." This has resulted in a clash of sorts between the veterans, who want to focus more on caring for patients, and the newcomers, who want to get everyone focused on the data—especially the financials.

With all the talk about health care reform (which, honestly, is a misnomer—the health care system is in a perpetual state of reform!), along with the continued changes in the reimbursement system these days, the notion of measuring the financial performance of a health care organization is all anyone seems willing to focus on. Listen, we're not here to argue against the reality that every organization needs to be financially viable so it has the resources to invest in its people and future vision. But we firmly believe getting to that point—achieving that financial viability—starts with a focus on employee engagement.

Take a quick peek at the cover of our book. In case you'd forgotten, the title is *Patients Come Second*. We applaud all of you who worked past your sense of recoil over that phrase to keep reading to this point. Now we can actually complete the equation by telling you that employees come first, patients come second, and—gasp!—financials come third.

"Wait a minute!" you might be saying. "You just said your company needs to be profitable to operate, so how come profitability is only third on your list?" Well, just as we posit that engaged employees will drive higher patient satisfaction, so too will the combination of high employee and patient measurements push profits higher. You need to add up the first two in order to achieve the third. The more our employees are engaged, the more satisfied our patients will be—which will then lead to more and more business for the organization. It's really that simple. Your financial performance is actually the lagging indicator, not the leading indicator, of how healthy your organization is.

Unfortunately, most health care organizations seem to have missed the memo on this crucial message. We were talking recently with one frustrated hospital CEO who told us that all her corporate board wants to focus on is making cuts to staff and equipment—controlling costs—as the way to get profits up. We felt for her, because if your job is simply to cut and trim, eventually you're going to hit bone and muscle. You're going to start chipping away at the structure that holds the organization together. That's no way to build toward your future.

Now, we're all taught that there are two primary ways to boost profit: cut costs and raise revenue. But for health care organizations, here's the rub: Because they must deal with a high percentage of variable costs, and because the complex reimbursement system restricts how much of that revenue actually stays in the hospital's hands, it's harder to get a lot of bang for your buck if you target revenues as the answer. That, of course, leaves cost cutting as the only option most executives consider viable.

Well, we're here to tell you that there are other avenues for health care organizations to take toward financial sustainability. And if people aren't open to walking down those paths, they're basically shooting themselves in the foot. In fact, we'll go out on a limb and use a four-letter word to describe organizations that focus just on cutting costs as a way to boost their financials: lazy. Yup—we said it. It's too easy to pull out a spreadsheet filled with revenues and costs and simply start deleting. That's not leadership—that's just math. We think everyone would agree that the better the members of a team or an organization work together, the better the results will be—but how do you measure something like that? Adding up costs is straightforward; it gets a bit murky when you try to think about measuring the experience of working together. Most people might not even know what it's like to work on a truly great team, so how would they know where to begin measuring that experience? Now you see why it seems so much easier just to cut something.

To borrow a line from the brilliant visionary behind computer giant Apple, the late Steve Jobs, our challenge to you leaders out there is to "think different." Shift your focus and turn your equation around—focus on your employees first, not your financials. Become accountable not just to your patients and your accountants, but to your employees—which means, as Tom Royer, past CEO of CHRISTUS Health, defines it, "You will do the best you can do, even when no one is looking." By doing your best to emphasize and support your employees, you'll drive your organization toward its mission, vision, and values.

"Okay, so if we take a chance and believe you," you might be asking now, "how are we supposed to go about measuring success with this new equation?" Good question. For any organization, measurement becomes a critical activity to determine whether you are continuing on the right path. It's a validation of everything you are striving for, and it gives people in the organization confidence that you are, indeed, heading in the right direction. If you can show that your organization has the best patient satisfaction scores, for instance, all your associates can point to that number with pride. Well, as long as you're being honest about when the numbers aren't as good, too, cautions John Hill, CEO of Medical Center of Aurora:

> Employees always sniff out the "spin" on patient satisfaction results. Always share the good results and bad results without spin. Celebrate improving and great results, and talk frankly about poor or negatively trending results. If the expectation has been set to achieve the ninetieth percentile in patient satisfaction results, talk about the bad results in the context of what is expected, and what is being done to improve the results and achieve the expected results. Never speak publicly in a punitive tone about the results, but nor should you cover up or spin negative results—this moves away from accountability and toward apathy. Employees want to achieve success, and when we've shared negative results in a frank and authentic way, the response of our employees has always been positive.

Positive or negative, metrics are important for looking back at your track record. But measuring also acts as an early-warning system so that if you do find yourself going off

track—say, if you see a steep decline in employee engagement or patient satisfaction scores—you can correct your
course before you really get lost in the desert. As much as
we'd like to think that we could live our lives simply by listening to our gut, the truth is that we really do need data
and measurements to give us our bearings, the coordinates
of where we might be at any given point in time. Any organization can make strategic changes (tied to its mission,
vision, and values) in just about any area it wants to if you
begin measuring the kind of change you want to bring about.

START BY ASKING

At our organizations, measuring starts internally with our
annual employee engagement surveys, in which we ask
employees to answer questions using a scale that runs from
1 to 10. We've talked to executives at other organizations
who have told us that while they like the idea behind such
surveys, they've never gotten around to conducting them.
Big mistake. You know these same people made time to
review their organization's income statement and balance
sheets. Again, think different. If you believe that human
capital is your most valuable asset, how can you neglect
to gauge how well that asset is performing compared to
its potential? The answer is simple: to borrow another corporate tagline, "Just do it." Make the effort to start conducting regular employee satisfaction and engagement
surveys—you won't regret it.

Now, we'll go on record here and say that the term
satisfaction might be sending the wrong kind of message.
For us, it brings up images of Mick Jagger and the Rolling

Stones whining about how they can't get any. That's why it can seem as though when we conduct a satisfaction survey, we are catering to those individuals who are just never happy. *Engagement*, on the other hand, is a more powerful—and we think, accurate—term to use in this situation, because it implies that we are measuring who really cares about and likes working for the organization. To put that another way, we want to conduct these surveys not just to see who is happy or satisfied, but more to find out who cares about what we're doing together as a team.

That's why conducting engagement surveys becomes a fantastic tool to gauge whether we as an organization have any momentum or a sustainable trajectory to get us where we're headed. Are we working together to pick up operational speed and grow at a sustainable rate? Without momentum—we crash! Are we pointed in the right strategic direction? Wrong trajectory—let's pack it in, because we're done. And to understand our relative speed and course, it can be very helpful to then benchmark these survey results against other like-minded organizations. By comparing yourself to others, you'll give yourself a good dose of objective reality.

What's key for each of us and our organizations is this: By having the discipline to conduct the surveys regularly over time, we can analyze the patterns that emerge, patterns that can either give us reasons to celebrate progress or, on the other hand, to hit the pause button and find out where we're beginning to go wrong. We can then target the areas where we receive the lowest scores and set about trying to improve upon them.

BerylHealth, for instance, tackles the five lowest-scoring categories from the employee engagement survey by creating corresponding ten-person, cross-functional teams made up of leaders from throughout the company (anyone in a supervisory role), who then go about interviewing employees to determine why, say, they are pessimistic about the training and development they are receiving in their jobs. The leadership team tasked with that particular issue has thirty days to research and determine the problem and then another thirty days to come up with an action plan and to make recommendations about how the company can combat the problem.

We'll share a little tip with you: Make the time to look through each and every one of the survey comments. From experience, we have learned that this information is qualitative gold. It's a unique bridge into finding out what really makes your employees tick. This is something even the feared military leader General George S. Patton understood all too well. When it came to how his soldiers dressed, how they carried themselves on and off the battlefield, and even how they saluted, Patton was as old school as they came. But when it came to how those same soldiers named and decorated their tanks, well, Old Blood and Guts seemed to have a soft side: He allowed them to do pretty much whatever they pleased. When asked why, Patton simply replied that he got a better understanding of his men based on the graffiti they wrote. In other words, he understood the value of collecting both emotional data and factual data to fuel strategies that could effect change.

Now, the two of us can admit that making the

commitment to dive into all that emotional information your employees provide through their mini-essays can be both exhausting and, on occasion, depressing. Reading about all the bad things your employees think and feel not only about the workplace but also about you personally as a leader can really take a toll. Of course, the task at hand is not to identify who among the commenters might be the kinds of whiners, losers, and jerks you need to extricate from your organization. You can't simply write off every employee who makes a negative comment. What you can do is look for common themes and patterns that tell you it's not just one person piping up. Common themes and complaints point to common problems. And once you identify the issues, that's when you can start taking action.

MEASURE BY LISTENING

Effective measuring isn't just about conducting surveys. To truly get a handle on the satisfaction and engagement levels of your employees, you need to create multiple input channels for them to communicate with you. Sometimes just getting out and walking the hospital hallways is an opportunity for making that connection and learning about what makes your employees tick. "The more I can get out, and the more our leaders can get out and about, I think the better everybody feels about what we're trying to do to be the best at what we're doing," Mike Packnett, CEO of Parkview Health, told us. "And I get such great energy when I do it, too. You get so inspired."

In many ways, our role as a leader is to play the detective or an investigator you might see on a TV show like

CSI. Your survey data serves as the first clue in your investigation of how well your organization is really functioning. It's not enough, however, just for everyone to say that the organization has a great culture; you've got to be willing to dig deeply into other clues and to use other methods to conduct your investigation.

At BerylHealth, for instance, we've told you before about the intranet link "Ask Paul," where employees can submit comments and opinions. Paul also uses another channel (an idea stolen from Britt), holding what he calls Chat-and-Chews, where he meets with employees over lunch to get them to share their ideas and concerns. Steve Moreau, CEO of St. Joseph's Hospital of Orange, has created his own version of the Chat-and-Chew, which he described for us:

> I have a monthly breakfast for frontline staff and each department in the hospital. There are almost one hundred departments. Each department selects one employee to meet with me and have a monthly breakfast with me for a period of six months. Their job, or their free ticket to come to the CEO breakfast each month, is that they solicit questions, issues, rumors, anything they can come up with, and they e-mail them to me in advance. When I come to the meeting, I answer all their questions, regardless of what they are—tough ones, easy ones, whatever— all in front of the whole group. I then answer questions from the group if there are new ones, and provide updates if there's anything going on that they might want to hear

about. Then all of it is published so that the whole organization gets to hear it.

By holding these kinds of sessions, as a leader you show that you're truly receptive to the needs and issues that are important to your people. You're on the path to making better decisions because you have gained access to true, actionable data that you won't find on any financial statement. That's not to say that collecting information this way is always easy. Britt recalls a time when he organized a Chat-and-Chew for a group of employees who, in a recent satisfaction survey, were in the bottom 10 percent—those with the biggest complaints. He wanted to find out how to right the ship for them. After an hour of nodding his head at the flood of negative comments, Britt realized his mistake: He needed to embed some positive thinkers along with the negative ones. For the next Chat-and-Chew, he invited an equal number of low and high scorers to set the tone for the conversation. The effect was immediate: The conversation stayed focused on the changes that would really bring about a difference rather than just the comments voiced by a complainer.

This reveals how important it is to recognize the crucial role your star employees play as role models for your less stellar employees. The superstars effectively become ambassadors for the mission, vision, and values of the organization even when you, the leader, aren't there. That's something that can be reinforced by building a process or a system around this whole idea. Elliot Joseph, CEO of Hartford

Healthcare, told us about just such a program he created, called How Hartford Healthcare Works (or H3W), which has since been implemented across his organization:

H3W requires that every employee is a member of a work group, and every work group has regular meetings at least once a month. Every work group has a leader, and we have created a group of facilitators who are trained in the H3W work, in change management, in the tools of change management—whether it be Lean or Six Sigma, or whatever might be in the toolbox that gets embedded in how you improve. Each work group is data driven, has its own dashboard, and is driven by our trained facilitators, who facilitate multiple work groups. The program is based on teamwork and recognition, so every team meeting has all those aspects of the team meeting.

You can now go across the organization and understand, in every work group, what their priorities are, what they're measuring, how they're improving. It's about idea generation in every work group, so we've generated thousands upon thousands of ideas from seven thousand people—now today at Hartford Healthcare, fifteen thousand people—with literally hundreds and hundreds of those ideas having been implemented and executed upon. At the same time, the work group is also a vehicle for communication, so when we have system-wide or organization-wide initiatives to introduce, now there's an organized framework through H3W to actually execute new initiatives. So you can walk into virtually any department, any work group, and you can ask people who work there, what are their priorities? What are they measuring? What are they implementing? And they have very visible dashboards in place, and it's almost an entirely different world for people.

When you bring your employees together to exchange ideas, you open up a channel of communication by speaking to them in the language of change—and they have a voice with which to respond.

You also need to understand the importance of who shouldn't speak when you gather your employees to collect information. When Britt holds his employee forums, those gatherings where employees assemble to get the latest updates on the organization, the hospital's chief financial officer doesn't go through a rundown of the organization's financials. This report is a given in most other organization forums, whether they operate in the health care field or not. The point in striking the financials from the list of topics is not to disrespect the importance of the numbers; it's to emphasize that there are other things that we should focus on first.

This gets back to our earlier point about the importance of your mission, vision, and values. If the CFO is the only one talking about the financials, then it seems like that dirty word *profit* is reserved for only the bean counters. Sometimes those of us who work in the health care field can get on our high horses and spurn discussions of the financials. We act as though we should be more interested in patient care and worrying about the bottom line is such a nuisance. Really? Think about it—we're still operating a business here. It's like when you bring up the topic of how everyone needs to watch expenses, and you see a couple of people roll their eyes. You want to reach out and grab them and ask, "How do you like your paycheck?" That would get their attention, right? But what we're talking about goes beyond this simple point. We have a moral obligation to be wise stewards of the sacred resources we've been entrusted with. Patients and families are struggling to pay their health care bills, which means we have the responsibility to be as efficient and effective as we can be. We owe that to our patients and our communities.

So when the time comes to hold employee forums and gatherings, it makes sense to invite everyone on the team—CEO, CFO, CNO, whatever—so that we can talk about all the measures we track throughout the organization. Ron Swinfard, CEO of Lehigh Valley Health System, whose organization has 11,500 total employees, has conducted employee forums for as many as six thousand employees. "We invite literally everyone," he said. "Housekeepers, service workers, new residents, EMS providers, et cetera. We don't miss anyone. When people come here for care, they don't discriminate. They experience and get a feel for the everyday people when they come to the hospital."

When you start getting everyone involved, interesting things begin to happen. You can have a cool experience like watching a CFO speak with passion about the importance of employee engagement. That means he gets it! He understands that the success of the organization must be measured not just in financial terms but also through patient loyalty, physician satisfaction, performance quality, and yes, employee engagement. Rulon Stacey, a renowned health care executive and former chairman of the American College of Healthcare Executives, and a past winner of the Malcolm Baldrige National Quality Award, put it this way:

> The biggest challenge on our road to Baldrige was to infuse a sense of responsibility by leaders, a duty to listen to the team and then embrace what they were being told. It requires courage and commitment to the mission, vision, and values of the organization.

Business schools may churn out executives skilled at identifying an organization's key performance indicators (KPIs) as a way to measure success. But when the CFO gets up on stage during an employee forum to discuss employee engagement and patient satisfaction scores—well, you get quite a reaction from the crowd. The employees might be expecting a numbers-crunching session, but hearing the organization's chief financial executive speak instead with passion and personality only helps to emphasize what's most important to the success of the organization: employees. Sure, you need to collect all the data and KPIs to get a holistic view of how you are operating. But if the data isn't what's driving you toward your ultimate goals, don't emphasize it. If that kind of data is becoming a distraction more than a tool, then stop collecting it.

CELEBRATE YOUR VICTORIES

As a leader, you will periodically ask management to review the progress and measure the health of your organization. But when people spend their time analyzing quantitative data rather than focusing on the human side of things, they seem to forget the changes and achievements the organization has made since the time you last asked them. You might catch yourself saying, "Are you kidding me? Don't you remember what we did to address that problem?" While you can give in to some frustration, ask yourself why your people have forgotten. Have you done enough to communicate and celebrate the victories that your organization has experienced? That is, have you found ways to effectively take credit for the changes you have put in place as your employees asked?

Remember our football example? People like to associate with winners and organizations that see continued success on their journey toward the mountaintop. You need to find ways to show them that both they and the organization are winning when it comes to things that go beyond the financials. You need to confirm the emotional victories along with the factual ones. That's why, returning to the BerylHealth example, the leadership teams tasked with recommending changes based on their research are also asked to report back to the rest of the organization at the end of the year about what progress, if any, was made to address each concern. The key idea here is that you as the CEO or leader don't have to own the sole burden of dealing with that data. Open it up and share with everyone in the organization so that all of you can work together as a team to tackle your weaknesses and celebrate your achievements.

It's also critical to seek and call attention to external validation that chronicles what you as an organization have accomplished. Consider how Paul and Britt met: on stage, as recipients of the Best Place to Work awards sponsored by the *Dallas Business Journal*. Ah, you skeptics are raising your hands again, aren't you? "Those kinds of awards are just beauty contests," you might be saying. "They don't mean anything." We disagree. In fact, we contend that winning awards like these is a way to both measure and celebrate the success of your organization. And as we noted earlier about football fans, everyone likes to be part of a winning team.

Awards like these function as directional signposts that indicate successes along the path to the mountaintop. By celebrating achievements in employee engagement, we are communicating both our interest in the employee and the value of the employee experience. But don't just take our word for it. Give it a try. Create an internal award that celebrates the performance of one of your teams. Bang the drum loud and proud! We bet that, all of a sudden, you'll see other teams scrambling to be recognized as well.

Britt saw this kind of explosion when, at Presby, he helped put together a funny music video celebrating the departments that received the best employee engagement scores. Wouldn't you know it? After that, other teams came calling, asking why they weren't being celebrated too. Well, once we told them that recognition was linked to their engagement scores, you should have seen the stampede! Everyone wanted to be a part of a winning team.

But you shouldn't stop at celebrating employee engagement scores; other metrics are just as powerful. When Britt was at Medical City, for example, he posed a question to his senior leadership team: "How do you celebrate the success of the folks who work in your unit?" At first, he received little more than blank stares in response. Other than noting daily productivity and adherence to budgets, no one had ever thought about how to celebrate the successes their unit achieved. But when Britt asked them to put together a list of the kinds of activities that everyone could measure—in both quantitative and qualitative terms—you could feel the energy being generated inside the room.

The results were electric! Britt's leadership team found ways to celebrate, for example, the success of the respiratory therapy department in its recent quiz show victory—a regional event known as the Sputum Award. (We know, we know—it sounds kind of gross!) The finance team often struggled to find ways to reduce costs and improve processes, so they created the Bright Idea Awards. Not only did this program inspire numerous initiatives, but the team also put together a hilarious video highlighting the accomplishments of several clever team members. The video was a hit at the next employee forum series, and the award recipients—the stars of the video—beamed with pride.

Collectively, the units at Medical City saw great results when the organization received recognition from an external source, becoming one of the first hospitals in Texas (and one of four hundred out of the nation's six thousand hospitals) to be designated by the American Nurses Association as a Magnet hospital—a prestigious accomplishment that signifies the hospital is on the cutting edge of delivering high-quality care. Winning this award wasn't just a chance for the organization and its employees to celebrate what they had accomplished; it also served as an incredible benefit in terms of talent, drawing top-notch nurses around the country who wanted to come work for such an organization. At first, no one thought Medical City could win the award. Now, Dallas is the home to the highest concentration of Magnet hospitals precisely because other organizations in the area had to raise the bar to keep up with Medical City.

Do you see how celebrating your organization's victories becomes a self-fulfilling cycle? It's kind of like throwing the life preserver farther and farther out and then challenging your team to swim as hard and as far as they can. Winning an accolade like Magnet recognition becomes a way to measure how far you've come—and serves as inspiration for others to follow your lead. The more we celebrate our successes, the more successful we—not just as an organization, but also as a community—become in the future.

That brings us back to the key point of this chapter and of the book in general: Measuring your employee satisfaction and engagement level is the leading indicator of how healthy your organization really is. Higher scores here translate into higher patient satisfaction scores and better financial performance. It's as simple as connecting the dots. Measuring how engaged your employees are—and finding ways to celebrate the successful changes you implement—is how you can connect back to driving the mission, visions, and values of your organization. Developing recognition that your team can work toward helps you as a leader determine what goals you need to hit in order to stay on track toward fulfilling your ultimate purpose. So what are you waiting for? Get started!

But how? Join us in the next chapter to find out.

CHAPTER EIGHT

It Ain't About the Money

After all our discussion, the importance of recognizing and rewarding the achievements of your staff should come as somewhat of a no-brainer: You know you need to do it. Duh. The harder question becomes, therefore, how do you do it well? The mistake many leaders make is that they lean back on some kind of cookie-cutter approach to implementing recognition. No matter what you think, there is no one-size-fits-all solution you can buy off the shelf. And turning to something as mundane as handing out employee-of-the-month plaques won't cut it either. This is something you're going to have to figure out on your own, according to the needs of your particular organization, and you're going to have to use some creativity. As Tony Armada, CEO of Advocate Lutheran General Hospital, told us, "If you want to treat people like just employees, they'll be just employees. If you want to treat them the best, to reward and recognize them, they'll be engaged."

You've made it this far, folks, so now is not the time to start acting lazy. Yes, perhaps we're taking a none-too-subtle shot at the canned, turnkey solutions and easy promises offered by the various consulting organizations out there. We know, they can make those solutions sound tempting. But we can tell you from experience that unless you approach the topic of rewards and recognition with purpose and personalization, where you make the effort to acknowledge an individual's effort in a very personal, nonhomogenized way, you're almost guaranteed to fail. It's not something to be done sporadically, either—you're going to have to commit to acknowledging your people regularly.

And what if you don't? Put simply, trying to fake praise is a great way to create disengagement among your employees. You have to get it right, or they'll see right through your weak efforts. There's no doubt that the process of doling out rewards and recognition is more of an art than a science. But regardless, it's something you need to be doing—now. Melody Trimble, CEO of Sparks Health System, explained it to us like this:

> How do you recognize people who are doing well? First it has to be genuine. Second, it should be unexpected. I ask people when they start with us to fill out a survey to tell me how they like to be recognized. I'm a big card person. Everyone tells me I should have stock in Hallmark.

We know, we know—not everyone is going to buy into this. Remember Britt's CFO colleague we discussed in chapter two, the one who thought employee engagement has nothing to do with the financials? Not surprisingly, he didn't believe in employee recognition and reward programs either. "Once you start doing that, people will expect to be rewarded more and more," this CFO (let's call him

"Mr. Pennypincher") once told Britt. "When will it ever stop?" The answer, of course, is that it won't ever stop. This isn't something where you can just check a box and say, "Whew, glad that's done." No, this is a commitment you need to make that will continually tie your organization back to its mission, vision, and values.

We also need to acknowledge that if you are new to your organization and want to bring these kinds of changes to it, you might need to start slowly. We know how difficult it can be to parachute into an existing organizational culture and try to bring big new ideas into play right off the bat. That means taking it one step at a time and building slowly based on what works. You want to build the kind of engaged workforce most leaders can only dream of, and getting a vibrant, effective rewards and recognition program in place is a big piece of the puzzle.

DON'T SHOW ME THE MONEY

Let's take a step back and make a key point: Most people aren't motivated by money alone. This means that simply handing out bonuses or some such is not the only way people want to have their hard work rewarded. Let's face it: We're all hardwired to crave a pat on our shoulder for a job well done. But when you actually combine that individual recognition with an object—something as simple as a trophy or a plaque, embedded with some connection to your organization's purpose—the recipient of the award can then bask in the recognition he or she receives from peers and coworkers by displaying that trophy in the person's office or cubicle.

Case in point: Every time he holds a senior leadership meeting, Britt hands out what he has come to call Berrett's Carrots. These are three small Beanie Baby–like toy carrots he gives out to acknowledge people who have engaged in small acts of kindness—an idea inspired by the book *The Carrot Principle: How the Best Managers Use Recognition to Engage Their People, Retain Talent, and Accelerate Performance* by Adrian Gostick and Chester Elton. The central theme of the book is that organizations perform better and achieve better financial results when managers offer frequent, constructive praise and meaningful rewards that motivate employees to excel. What's interesting about this concept is that bestowing such awards doesn't always have to be linked to the things we're accustomed to recognizing in the business or the health care world, such as meeting budget or completing projects.

There's room here to be creative and reward even the smallest achievements with your own version of Berrett's Carrots that can mean more than you can ever imagine. Britt finds random opportunities to express appreciation for some efforts that may seem at first glance to be insignificant but that are, in fact, the small acts that make up the fabric of the organization. On one occasion, when a payroll clerk received an award accompanied by some comments of recognition from the president, she burst into tears, not realizing that her efforts were so greatly appreciated. Another time, Britt was walking down the hall of the hospital when he noticed one of his senior managers bend down and pick up a piece of garbage that was lying on the floor. Sure, maybe most people would have done the same thing. But at their next meeting Britt took the opportunity to acknowledge the good deed by handing this gentleman one of his carrots—something, for what it's worth, that manager proudly displays on his desk to this day.

And that brings up another interesting point: If you, too, want to find a powerful symbol of recognition to hand out, take a look at how your people decorate their offices and cubicles. If they love hanging their diplomas and certificates on their walls, that might be a clue as to how they like to be recognized. The same goes for tchotchkes and knickknacks; it's amazing the effect a stuffed carrot can have on employee motivation. Make the time to assess how your direct reports like to be recognized, and you'll find that those rewards bestow much more personalized recognition than you might ever imagine.

Take notice, too, that it often means a great deal to an employee to receive an accolade like a Berrett's Carrot in front of his or her peers. BerylHealth uses its annual holiday party to celebrate the winner of two major awards the company bestows each year. One is called the Barry Spiegelman Spirit Award, named for Paul's brother and BerylHealth business partner, who passed away in 2005. Barry was a fun-loving guy who brought an unbelievably positive spirit with him every day of his life, including throughout his fight with cancer. BerylHealth employees nominate their peers based on these values. The other major award is called the Face of BerylHealth, which recognizes someone for living the company's core values in a way that stands out from everyone else. This award is a beautiful glass sculpture that is prominently displayed in a case at the office for one year, to remind everyone who won the award and why, before the winner takes it home.

Remember, it's not the size of the award or even whether it's made of precious metals or a stuffed sock. It's the notion that the award means something special and all your people know it. Unfortunately, this is a notion that many of today's leaders can't wrap their head around. For instance, Paul met up with a fellow CEO who runs a large call center company. "I read your book, and our company is different, just like yours," the CEO said. Then he talked about how he created a bonus program that rewards his call advisers with a free lunch at a restaurant of their choice whenever they meet a certain quota of sales calls. All Paul could do was nod his head politely while he silently seethed, thinking, that is exactly *not* what we do at BerylHealth.

The idea is not to construct financial rewards based on some operational data, like the number of calls somebody makes. If you do that, your employees can see that you're just paying them to make you more money. People don't just want more money—they want to feel valued. That's our message here, our challenge to you leaders out there: Break free from what you think leadership means, and think differently about what it means to nurture long-term financial sustainability. To stay on board for the long haul, you need to get out of your short-term focus on reaping immediate ROI and begin to see the bigger picture—the reality that only when you have successfully engaged your employees can you really experience long-term success and viability.

MAKE IT MEANINGFUL

We can't stress enough how important it is to make your reward and recognition program meaningful and purposeful in some way. For a while now we've been talking up rewards handed down by your boss or upper management, but there's one thing that trumps this sort of recognition: receiving acknowledgment from your peers. This isn't referring just to peers and coworkers handing out the occasional "Thanks!" for a job well done. You as a leader can help institutionalize that kind of recognition by creating a program similar to BerylHealth's PRIDE program (Peers Recognizing Individual Deeds of Excellence), which we discussed in chapter two. The idea behind this program is simply to give employees a chance to recognize one another in a very powerful and public way. The way it works is this: BerylHealth employees use the company intranet to nominate coworkers who live up to one of BerylHealth's five core values. The process is easy; they simply have to type in the person's name along with a few sentences describing how the individual exemplifies one of those values. Then, at every quarterly meeting, which for us has the feel of a town hall meeting, all the nominations are placed in one of five hats (one for each core value) and a name is chosen from each. The prize for winning is $250.

We know what you're probably saying: "But that's a financial reward!" True, but it comes with a catch. Before the drawing, each nominee has to write down what he or she intends to do with the money if in fact that person wins the prize. The point is, we want the winners to do something special with that money, not just fill their gas tank or pay their rent. The stakes are raised even further because winners then have to take a picture of whatever they buy, like a new outdoor grill or dinette set, and post it back on the company intranet as a way to share the celebration and have some fun with the award.

Putting an organization-wide program like PRIDE in place is also a way to empower your employees to recognize the accomplishments of their peers in—get this—other departments. Let's face it: Most organizations are built with internal walls, and we mean this both literally and figuratively. In a large hospital there might be, say, thirty departments that can influence a patient's experience. The truth is, however, most departments don't really know what the other ones are doing to positively influence the nature of a patient's stay. Wayne Lerner, CEO of Holy Cross Hospital, put it like this:

> In health care, we go through our education in silos. Then we graduate and they throw us together in a patient care environment and ask us to go work together. That's why you need a unifying theme.

With programs that encourage employees to be aware of and take an interest in what's going on in the organization's other "silos," we can be sure we are doing all we can to foster our company culture and improve the patient experience.

At Britt's hospital, for example, they have implemented a program called the Traveling Trophy. Each department

nominates someone from another department for performing an exemplary deed. The winners of the award get to
display the trophy in their department. Often the winning
team members are so delighted about their accomplishment,
they add a little extra flair to show off how proud they are. It
begins with a ceremony announcing the recipients in front
of the leadership team, followed by a brief expression of recognition. But some recipients are so excited that they take
the microphone and practically gush with enthusiasm and
appreciation for the award! By putting the power to reward
and recognize into the hands of his department heads, Britt
has found a way for cross-functional teams to highlight and
recognize all the important tasks and actions each department takes in creating those amazing patient experiences.

Presby reinforces this principle by holding a Support
Services Fair every quarter. The idea here is to give those
departments that aren't always seen on the patient-facing
front lines—security, quality control, housekeeping, and
such—a chance to explain what they do for their peers in
other departments. This paves the way for these groups to
get credit for doing a great job at what they do.

When recognition of your people comes from outside
the walls of the organization, with local, regional, even
national acknowledgment, showing your support can be
the icing on the cake. For example, the annual program 100
Great Nurses brings winners of this prestigious distinction
up on stage at a big gala event to receive their reward.
Britt's organizations have always made it a point to bring
as many people as possible to those events, so when one
of the winners from their hospital walks across the stage,

they can unleash the cowbells, air horns, and clappers to create all the noise they can muster. Can you imagine how good it feels for someone to have their peers celebrating their award by going berserk for them in front of a packed auditorium? Wow.

At Britt's organization, the hospital staff also take pains to acknowledge the efforts of its physicians. Okay, okay—you're probably saying something like, "Doctors get thanked by their patients all the time. They've got support from all the other hospital workers. How needy are these people anyway?" Ah, but there's the rub. All too often, as we discussed in chapter six, physicians seem to be in conflict with the very colleagues—nurses, orderlies, staff—who are charged with supporting them. Think about the power of an award of recognition, therefore, that comes directly from those peers. That's why Presby holds an all-star reception every quarter, where two physicians who have been nominated by the hospital's employees are recognized for exceptional work. What's amazing about these luncheons is that almost without fail, the physicians receiving the awards bring their spouses and their office staff along with them to the event. Receiving this kind of recognition from their peers across the hospital means a lot to these men and women, so naturally they want to share the honor with their loved ones and coworkers. Can you see the power in this culture of appreciation and respect? Can you see how this might impact how that physician reflects on his or her relationships with the rest of the staff and with the organization as a whole?

The same principle holds true for any position in the

health care field, of course. That means you have to think holistically when it comes to whom you involve in your reward and recognition programs. For example, at Beryl-Health, there was clearly a need to recognize the efforts of the patient experience advocates—the men and women on the front lines, fielding all the phone calls that drive the business. These folks are so important to the success of the company that Paul has turned the entire organizational chart upside-down, so these people sit at the top while he is at the bottom, because it's his job to support them in their efforts. In this case, recognition is built into the everyday structure of the organization.

The problem BerylHealth ran into, however, was that the people in between—the support staff, the human resources department, the sales teams, and so forth—began to feel neglected. Heck, the bulk of their job may involve sending e-mail and tracking numbers, but that doesn't mean these people don't want their hard work acknowledged as well. So the PRIDE program has helped BerylHealth support the employees who support the frontline folks. It works for Paul and his people: You'll need to figure out how best to spread the love within your own organization.

The key takeaway is this: It is critical to develop reward and recognition programs that touch everyone in the organization in meaningful ways. No, you shouldn't give someone a trophy just because she sends e-mail. But when you can find a way to reward your people for extra efforts—like when they help organize a bake sale for an ailing coworker or take the time to notice details like trash in the hall-ways—well, then you're really onto something.

GET CREATIVE

Of course, regardless of how expansive you try to make your reward and recognition program, you'll always end up with someone who feels as though he or she didn't get the appreciation he or she deserved. It might even be you. After all, it can be easy to overlook the efforts of a leader, especially if that person is attempting to till new ground.

Well, if you find yourself in this predicament, or you are approached by one of your employees who feels this way, take a deep breath and give yourself a brief time-out. The solution is right in front of you: Simply find a way to recognize the efforts of someone else instead. Yes, pay it forward by appreciating the effort made by someone else and—poof!—your own hard feelings will magically evaporate. Counsel your managers in the same way. Do they feel unappreciated? Well then, make a list of which team members are performing the best on their team and find a way to recognize their efforts. Not only will this make you feel better in the short term, it also has a funny way of coming back around to you over the long haul.

Here's something else to consider: People also respond in powerful ways, as we discussed in chapter five, when they get recognized for things they care about outside the four walls of the organization. For example, one hospital executive told us about a program he had dubbed Mission Time Off: everyone in the organization is given one week a year, with pay, to give back to their community in some manner. Then, when they get back to work, they give a presentation to their peers, celebrating what they've accomplished in their time away from the office. How powerful is that—to not just give back to your community but also to get all your peers hooting and hollering as they celebrate what you have accomplished?

Recognizing your people for a passion they have outside work can be a powerful way to encourage engagement with the organization. For example, one hospital executive told us that she posts an eight-by-ten photograph of every employee along one hallway of the hospital—and each employee gets to choose his or her own photo, as it's supposed to represent whatever the individual's passion is. So, as you walk down this hallway, you might see people ballroom dancing or completing a marathon or holding up the blue ribbon for their homemade apple pie.

The folks at the Medical Center of Plano take a similar approach when it comes to posting photos of the hospital's past presidents. Rather than those standard, all-too-serious head shots with some guy or gal in a suit, you'll see twenty years' worth of presidents posing with their piano, their fly-fishing gear, or their cowboy hat. (For what it's worth, Britt's photo would be of him driving his 4x4 Jeep through a mud pit, while Paul's would show him serving up an ace to his tennis opponent.) What a cool way for people to show their peers who they really are—to help them connect with and admire one another for their various passions and accomplishments. That's especially true when you compare this practice to the boring employee-of-the-month photos you see from time to time. Sure, it's a way to recognize someone, but it's not all that inspirational. Step it up, folks! Have some fun with this whole recognition thing.

COMPLETE THE CIRCLE

Now that we've explored some of the do's and don'ts of driving internal recognition for your team, it's time to look at the power that comes when your team receives external recognition—especially from the communities that surround you. It's important not to neglect this aspect of acknowledging your people. Getting recognized by people in your community has real value and brings a tremendous amount of pride to everyone involved. Imagine you run into an old friend or neighbor at the grocery store, and he or she asks what you're doing these days. You tell him or her that you work at BerylHealth or Medical City or Texas Health Presbyterian Hospital, and the friend says something like, "Oh, yeah? I've heard of them—that's a great place to work. I'm so jealous!" Believe us, it gives you a real boost to hear such words. Quite simply, it feels good.

So why not create a process that spreads the word about your employees' accomplishments and victories? Finding ways to share these stories with your colleagues reinforces everyone's sense of pride in the organization. When BerylHealth holds its employee forum every month, one of the agenda items is Kudos, and people get the chance to acknowledge good deeds performed throughout the company. Just as important, though, is another agenda item that allows people to take the time to share their stories about customers praising the company and the brand throughout the community.

We've found that the most fun stories to share involve cases where people ended up getting a job at BerylHealth because of non-BerylHealth employees touting it as a great place to work. A guy working at a local Kinko's, for instance, was talking to a UPS guy during a delivery and mentioned that he was looking for something better, the next step in his career; after the UPS guy told him about BerylHealth, he was hired a few weeks later. We got great service from a guy in the Verizon store and hired him on the spot. We even hired an employee whose mother was in the hospital and heard from the other patient in the room that Beryl-Health was a great place to work. We get a real kick out of hearing stories like that; they build pride in what we're all trying to do together: create a workplace that is second to none.

Up next, we'll discuss the key role that training and development play in building an engaged workforce and making sure that special workplace becomes a reality.

CHAPTER NINE

Committing to a Lifetime of Learning

Here's an interesting question for you to ponder: Which position requires more continual training and development in order to perform at a high level—a dental hygienist or a hospital executive? No, it's not a trick question. The answer is the hygienist, who, like nurses and other caregivers, is required to invest a certain number of hours each year in continuing his or her education. That makes sense, of course; you'd like to think that the people caring for patients are skilled in the latest and greatest techniques and technology out there. There is no mandate, though, that requires executives to keep improving their management or communication skills. Does that seem strange to you? Shouldn't administrators be pushed into continually developing and evolving their skills, too? We sure think so.

This is something that particularly hits home for Britt, whose wife is a dental hygienist. To Britt's credit, however, he has pushed himself to keep learning, both by pursuing his PhD (while working full-time) and by joining the American College of Healthcare Executives—the only professional association around that caters to health care administrators. In other words, whether he was required to do so or not, Britt saw the value in continuing his education—something he pursues to this day.

Paul, too, is familiar with the impulse to continually further his education. When he finished law school, he knew he wasn't headed for a career as an attorney; rather, he was working with his brothers to start a company of their own. Unfortunately, there is no such thing as going to CEO school. So Paul turned to books written by the great business leaders of the day as a way to carve out a learning track for himself. Just as important, he also identified some of those leaders as mentors, hoping to shorten his own learning curve—something we'll come back to in more detail later in the chapter.

We know there are other executives out there who expect to spend a lifetime seeking learning and wisdom. In general, though, we feel that the health care field hasn't done enough to emphasize training and learning among its leadership. Other leaders in the industry, like Jim Hinton, CEO of Presbyterian Healthcare Services, share this feeling:

> I think health care has been a little reluctant to embrace training by saying, "Hey, here's how we do it." We've sort of assumed that if you have a doctor from Johns Hopkins and a nurse from University of Chicago and a physical therapist from Cedars-Sinai, and they're all working together in one room, they all must know the best practices for taking care of that patient. Well, they don't, because they were all trained in different places.

I think the same thing applies to beliefs about management. We sort of let people manage the way they want to manage. That's an opportunity for us to grow. We firmly believe that leaders must grow and develop through both experience and education in its many forms. Clinicians and caregivers must seek new information and bring new skills and perspectives to the organization—why not the executives and administrators who lead that organization?

BREAK FREE FROM THE BOX

Going back to school—or at least exposing yourself to new ideas and skills, like knowing how to manage—should be an imperative for just about everyone out there, whether you are required to or not. Everyone should make a commitment to becoming a lifelong learner. That's how we make new leaps in our personal evolution, maybe in ways we never thought possible. Think about the story of the late Steve Jobs and how a class in calligraphy he took in his single year of college shaped the future success of Apple. After taking that class and immersing himself in a unique art form, Jobs made sure Apple always had a wide array of beautiful fonts available for its software—something that became a key differentiator in the company's early battles with Microsoft and other competitors.

"So what does that have to do with those of us who work in health care?" you might be asking. Well, just about everything. Your job as a leader is not only to commit yourself to a lifetime of learning but also to create the kind of culture where everyone you work with pushes themselves to do the same. That means creating new frameworks and opportunities for the people you work with to expand their own view of the world around them—and quite possibly to see new opportunities they wish to pursue.

That's why, while it might seem strange on the surface, the leadership team at Presby has participated in painting sessions and in conducting a symphony orchestra as ways to get people to both think outside the box and inspire new ideas. And that's why Paul holds Saturday morning professional development sessions taught by members of BerylHealth's leadership team, where his employees can learn how to write a resume, conduct a job interview, or dress for success with a wardrobe bought from Walmart. It's amazing to see how many people, a number of them single moms who make about $30,000 a year, come in on their own time to take advantage of this opportunity to improve their skill set. People attend these sessions, which begin at 7:00 a.m., because they've never been taught these basic skills and they want to learn. Driven by a sense of pride in wanting to grow as a professional, they show up enthusiastic and ready to move forward.

"Wait a darn minute!" you might be saying. "Why would you help your employees learn skills that might lead to them getting another job?" Ah, don't you get it by now, grasshopper? We're on a mission to drive our employee engagement levels through the roof. Look, we know that our society as a whole has changed and that the notion of lifetime employment, where we all work for a single employer our entire lifetime, is a thing of the past. Most people today want the chance to grow and move. Why would we want to impede that? Rather, we want to inspire people so when they do go somewhere else, they make a big and important impact— and perhaps even remember us as part of their history and progress. This is about sending a message that we do, in fact, care about our employees' success—now and into the future, regardless of whether they happen to be working for us in our organization. And we can tell you that the pay-off is actually much higher in terms of employee retention rates, because when you make these investments in your people—as opposed to worrying about the threat of losing them—they appreciate what you're doing for them. In the end, many of them stay because of it.

If someone doesn't feel as though he or she is a fit within the organization, though, we're not only giving that person the tools to find a path to a better future, but we're also hoping the person will spread the same kind of thinking he or she has learned while working in our organization— kind of like a bee moving from flower to flower, germinating each one as it goes. That's what we call a true win-win-win scenario.

SOCIALIZE THE LEARNING PROCESS

Educating oneself can be a demanding task to undertake, especially if you've fallen out of practice; it's not unlike going to the gym to work out a set of muscles you have long neglected. Plus, to be effective, a training and development exercise has to be engaging and fun. As soon as it starts to feel static and boring, you'll just be spinning your wheels. That's why, if you can make education more of a social enterprise—one that helps you build a sense of camaraderie with your fellow students—you'll find the entire experience far more enriching. Steve Moreau, CEO of St. Joseph's Hospital of Orange, has explained how he empowers these kinds of interactions:

> We do something called "crew training." It's something we learned from the airline industry. There were a number of catastrophic events because of the authority gradient between the pilot and the crew, and a lack of communication within the cockpit. And we have a similar environment in our operating suites or our interventional areas. So we learned that crew training was fundamentally important, and I personally went through crew training. We require every single physician who comes onto our campus and does any procedural work, and all our nurses who do any kind of procedural work, to go through a whole crew-training program.
>
> One of the questions we ask physicians who join us is "How many of you have ever been in a learning environment with nurses at your side?" And almost none of them have ever raised their hand. And the nurses have never been in the same classrooms and learned together with physicians. They are very much isolated. This is a joint learning opportunity, where they learn how important it is to communicate with the people around them. The nurses are there to keep the doctors out of trouble; the nurses are there to keep the patient out of trouble. The physician needs to understand they've got a whole team that is designed to be able to support them. They need to respect that team, and they

need to involve the nurses in it. It has to do with acknowledging them; it has to do with eye-to-eye communication; it has to do with the time-out process and saying we're all here to accomplish this goal today.

Given the traditional barriers between physicians and support staff, then, when you go about creating training and development opportunities for your colleagues, make sure not to neglect ways you can build a social element into the experience. When Britt was at Medical City, for example, he created something called Medical City Dallas University and dubbed himself, of course, the "chancellor." To make it fun, the whole concept was played out with a sense of humor in mind; the other leaders were called "deans," and conference rooms were "lecture halls." The point, though, was to create an environment where people could have fun learning.

Every month Britt would invite a different guest speaker to discuss interesting topics. There were also opportunities to take the "class" on "spring break," so to speak, by taking a road trip: holding class on a rented boat in the middle of a lake or sharing some lessons learned while out on a golf course. In order to create a great learning environment, you sometimes have to get people out of their comfort zone—and away from their phones and beepers—as a way to help them really engage in the act of learning. The idea is to find unique and exciting ways to combine purposeful fun with education.

Similarly, Paul has built a training and development program at BerylHealth that has come to be called the

Dashboard of Leadership. The program, which BerylHealth has held eleven times, lasts for ten weeks and requires lucky participants from all across the organization to spend four hours every Wednesday working through exercises and the like. To enroll in the program, BerylHealth employees need to be nominated by their peers—something that is perceived as an honor by most participants. In this way, the program also functions as a reward and recognition tool—an experience many BerylHealth employees count among their highlights of working for the company. The sessions are taught by members of the leadership team, including Paul, so it also becomes a great way for leaders to connect with a wide cross section of the company's top performers.

The Dashboard program has also become a great learning tool for Paul. When he teaches his session on understanding the core values of the organization, he conducts an exercise during which he breaks up the group into four groups of three. Each group is asked to grab an easel and a piece of paper, and they are given forty-five minutes to sketch an oceangoing vessel—anything from a sailboat to a cruise liner to a submarine—that represents, in their opinion, the status of the company. What's more important than the shape of the vehicle they choose, though, is the condition that it's in. In other words, Paul is able to gauge how his employees perceive the state of the company—whether it's sailing along nicely or headed for a disastrous encounter with an iceberg.

What's interesting is that when Paul began conducting this exercise, BerylHealth was going through tough times—a reality that was reflected in the drawings made by the Dashboard participants at the time. In these drawings, the skies were dark and stormy and people were jumping ship. Competitors, drawn as sharks, circled the boats ominously. The level of creativity was amazing! Today, Paul can chart the progress of BerylHealth's growth by looking back at the eleven sets of drawings he has collected—one for each year of the Dashboard of Leadership. In addition to being a great social exercise for the participants, these drawings have been a valuable training tool for Paul to use each year. Thankfully, the skies are blue now and no one has jumped ship in quite a while.

Bob Kelly, president of New York–Presbyterian Hospital, has come up with another way to socialize the learning process:

> We have set up several programs—one is called Building Tomorrow's Leaders, where we took thirty high-performing managers and put them into an eighteen-month program. There are classes two days a month; participants get a project, they work in teams, and they're doing some other things. And I make it clear to the senior management team that I expect the thirty best people in the organization to be included in this program; you can nominate whomever you want, and if you didn't nominate anybody, that's okay. But don't come to me at performance time and say, "Joe's the best and he has to get a great raise."

What Bob was saying is this: If "Joe" is "the best," don't just give him more money—take advantage of his talent by helping him to take that next step. Rather than nominating

someone for a great raise, nominate him or her to become
a great leader. In other words, it's all about creating the
kind of culture that rewards those who are driven to keep
learning and improving.

Another tremendous way to build a social learning
experience is to foster the creation of book clubs within
your organization. The size and composition of such clubs,
and how you go about handing out assignments and discussing the books, depend a lot on your organization. At
BerylHealth, for instance, there are both leadership and
cross-functional book clubs. At Presby, on the other hand,
Britt has some seven clubs made up of fifteen participants
each. In either case, the idea is to pick pieces of literature—anything from *Who Moved My Cheese?* by Dr. Spen-
cer Johnson . . . to *High Five!* by Ken Blanchard (a personal
favorite of Britt's, who just happens to be a huge hockey
fan) . . . to *Why Is Everyone Smiling?* by (you guessed it)
none other than Paul Spiegelman.

While the content of the books is obviously an important part of holding a book club, often you reap the true
value of these experiences during the resulting conversations and dialogue between your colleagues. For instance,
when Britt invites book club members to his office to discuss the latest assignment, he finds the experience far
more educational when the participants begin to interact
and riff off one another's points rather than look to him for
guidance. Sure, he sometimes needs to set ground rules,
and when someone seems afraid to raise his or her hand,
Britt raises it for that person (by calling on him or her).
But that's okay. Once people begin to understand that they

have a voice and opinions to share, they begin to build off one another—often applying real experiences from work as "case studies" in order to make the book's points more compelling. And because these groups are often made up of people from different departments, the book group serves as a fantastic way to cross-populate and learn from different disciplines within the organization. Britt has also come up with a fun way to put an exclamation point on such events: Everyone in attendance signs each of the books, as a way for everyone to remember the experience and whom they shared it with.

Paul has instituted a book club for about seventy BerylHealth employees; participants are given about two months to finish a book. He also gives them three questions to answer after they've finished reading; the answers serve as the prompts for a discussion at the next BerylHealth employee forum. Here's the rub: If an employee didn't take the time to read the book and answer the questions, he or she can't attend the forum. You can guess who are the ones who don't want to participate by reading the book, right? The ones who don't want to attend the forum. And it's no surprise to discover they are the least engaged employees in the organization. What Paul has found, though, is that attending the meeting is seen by almost everyone as a reward and an opportunity, and guess what: A vast majority of the time, people are actually excited to read, learn, and participate in bringing about change and offering new ideas that stem from the exercise. They share answers and ideas generated by reading the book, and even use them to stimulate great dialogue at the forum meetings.

Conducting a book club, then, is really about imposing a certain kind of discipline on the organization, and in this effort, everyone from the individual to the organization as a whole wins.

CHOOSE A MENTOR

You see, we can't do it all alone, but by reaching up, down, and across the organization, we can strengthen the team as a whole. Here's a dirty little secret of the business world: Most people are either too shy, embarrassed, or something else altogether to ask a more experienced businessperson for help. That's a big mistake and a huge missed opportunity when it comes to personal development. The more an individual can expose him- or herself to people who have achieved success—and who are willing to share some of the lessons they learned along that path—the more that person has advanced his or her own cause.

The problem is that most people don't even ask. We know this from experience. When they talk to us, people often start with a preamble along the lines of "I know you're busy . . ." But you know what? We're not too busy to help people out. We, like many others out there, actually take great joy when someone reaches out for help, for advice, or (on the flip side) to serve as a mentor of sorts. It all starts with having the courage to ask. Maybe it's a selfish thing for us, because it really does feel good when someone asks us—so why not take the chance? And we can tell you from experience that the mentor relationship truly does benefit the people who reach out. When you have the chutzpah to ask a more seasoned leader for help, you'll reap unbelievable rewards.

Mentorship can exist in both formal and informal ways—but you need to make it clear to everyone in your organization that each person has an obligation to cultivate mentor relationships whenever possible. You, like Britt, might have a more formalized system in your hospital, where leaders of the next generation are essentially linked up with members of the senior leadership team and then given a curriculum of new skills to hone. This is a way to both create a sense of camaraderie and develop a succession plan for the leadership team. And don't forget to keep an eye out for those who mentor, too; they are the teachers and coaches who are building great teams. True leaders surround themselves with engaging and talented people—the high-potential individuals in your organization. Invite someone like this to your next meeting, and see how the person glows when you stoke his or her interest and confidence.

Developing mentor relationships can be an informal and opportunistic endeavor as well. Back in the 1990s, Paul's company was awarded a contract with a very large health care organization. The CEO had started that business with $150,000 and, in time, grew it into a $30 billion enterprise. Paul befriended the CEO during the course of their business relationship, which only lasted for three years. For some reason, though, they connected, and the CEO seemed to genuinely care and be curious about Paul's little business that had served his company.

This CEO's name was John—well, no, it wasn't, but that's what we'll call him—and he left that company in 1997. But Paul stayed in touch with him and would either call or write a couple of times a year. In 2005, Paul visited John with a specific problem: BerylHealth's unique employee-focused culture had resulted in a lack of accountability within the business, and Paul wanted to instill greater discipline in this area.

"Look, Paul," John said, knowing that Paul didn't have a formal advisory board. "Accountability starts with you. Why don't you take one of those mentors you have, write the person a check for $20,000, and ask him or her to hold you accountable." Paul thought about it for a few days. Then he took out his checkbook and wrote a check for $20,000, making it out to John. When he mailed it, he included a note that said "I want you to hold me accountable." John called Paul up and said he'd do it. After that, they would connect for ninety minutes every month, on the phone or in person, to run down a nine-point agenda that would cover updates on everything from the company goals and financials to its biggest challenges and opportunities. Every year, Paul continues to write John a check for $20,000 (which he doesn't need, but cashes nonetheless), and this informal mentorship has had an immeasurable impact on Paul's career and life.

Paul was willing to ask for help, to opt in to a relationship with a mentor, and he got it in spades. But the story doesn't stop there. A year after he signed that first $20,000 check, after Paul spoke to a group of MBA students at Baylor University in Dallas, he got a call from two entrepreneurs who had been in the audience and were starting up a self-serve yogurt business. He invited them to meet him in his office, where they filled him in on their plans. Paul gave them what advice he could. He also told them the story about John and the importance of mentors. A week later, Paul got a note from them in the mail, along with a check for $2,000 and a note that said "We want you to hold us accountable."

Paul was impressed by their creativity and honored to be asked. He never cashed the check but gladly offered to help. Then, about six months later, twin brothers, one of whom had heard Paul speak to his MBA class at Texas Christian University, asked to meet with Paul to talk about starting a nonprofit aimed at improving educational opportunities for young people. When the two met, Paul shared the stories of John and the frozen yogurt guys, and a week later—can you believe it?—he received a check for $20 with a note that said "We want you to hold us accountable too!"

The point here, other than the fact that the next check Paul receives will likely be for $2, is that when people achieve a certain level of success, they want to give back and share their experiences. That means it's time for you to make a list of your would-be mentors and start reaching out. After all, what's it going to cost you? Probably nothing—other than a little bit of your time and a few stories about your experiences. You see, those experiences can be extremely valuable to others, and you can't just hold that knowledge inside. We call it "the give and get"—we get value from our mentors, and in return agree to give back by acting as mentors to others.

So get your mentors in line and working for you, and commit to offering to do the same for others. It will be good for your business and good for your heart; it's all part of the

ethics of reciprocity, otherwise known as the Golden Rule.
And as you'll see when you turn the page to start the final
chapter, we think following the Golden Rule is at the very
core of employee engagement.

CHAPTER TEN
The Higher Power That Drives Us

You made it to the last chapter. Wow! You've stuck with us this far, and we'd like to reward you by taking you through some conclusions about what we've discussed so far—namely, why employee engagement matters so much, and how this topic has inspired us to take this journey with you.

First, though, a little story: A few years ago, Paul invited Britt to speak in front of a BerylHealth-sponsored conference in Dallas. A little time had passed since our original meeting, and the two of us were becoming fast friends, especially because we were both so passionate about the topic of employee engagement. Anyway, picture the scene: a room packed with people, everyone from senior executives to marketing and communications folks, all there to hear Britt talk. Before he did, though, Paul came up to the podium to introduce him. And, in between all the kind words he had to say about Britt, he kind of lost his way somewhat: While Paul meant to say that he and Britt shared a similar mind-set or even that they were kindred spirits, what he actually said was, "Britt and I are soul mates."

Now, fortunately this statement, which resulted in quite a few hoots and hollers that day, didn't get us in trouble with our wives. The truth is, though, that despite some merciless heckling in the years since, we have come to admit there is quite a bit of truth to Paul's statement—especially as it applies to the contents of the book you hold before you.

Ultimately, we sat down together to write this book because we want to change the world of health care. We're not the only ones on such a mission, of course. But in our opinion, there are thousands more of our "soul mates" out there who believe that employees should come first. These soul mates are seeking a voice that speaks to them and an opportunity to share their stories and rub shoulders with other like-minded leaders.

Let's face facts: Health care hasn't advanced as fast and as far as other industries in recent years. And maybe that's because of the serious consequences that come from making change when people's lives are at stake. We are facing some unimaginable challenges, and it's time to rethink how we go about running our health care organizations. It's time to consider doing things in a way that they have never been done before.

According to Wayne Lerner, CEO of Holy Cross Hospital, his son said it best:

> He was ten years old when he said, "Dad, I think I know how to succeed in business. It's all about the Golden Rule."
> I told him that he is exactly right. If you treat people like human beings, they'll give it back to you.

My dad died at fifty-nine. He was a small business-
man. He had an accounting firm. People would come into
his office and Dad could tell someone no, but they would
still shake his hand before they walked out the door. It's all
about how you were brought up.

And that's the Golden Rule: Treat someone how you would
like to be treated. That means we won't be able to fix the
problems in health care by homing in on the details of reimbursement, balance sheets, and cost cutting. These kinds of
technical tasks will always be a challenge, no matter what
kind of business you run. By looking at the financials alone
as the root of the problem, though, we're taking our eyes off
the real ball. We are forgetting to consider how we ought
to treat one another and how that might affect the success
of our business.

That's why we as an industry need to get back to the
basics of building employee engagement, driving core values, and pursuing what Paul and Britt call a "higher power."
To us, the phrase *higher power* means many things—everything from our spiritual faith to the love of our families and
friends to the deeper purpose we find in our work. Let's face
it: Working in health care is hard. You need to put in too
many hours for too little pay. But that doesn't keep people
from being drawn to it. Choosing a career in health care is
about much more than how big your paycheck is and how
hard you have to work. You choose this field only if helping people fits into your personal purpose, if you feel that
giving back shapes your legacy and what you leave behind.
Steve Moreau, CEO of St. Joseph's Hospital of Orange,

describes the motivation to work in health care as a series of "sacred encounters":

> Sacred encounters is a description of the kind of experience we want people to feel when they're here with us. But those experiences don't come from a religious perspective per se. They come from trying to describe a deeper connection with people, trying to make a difference not only to our patients but also in how people treat one another.

That's why health care executives and workers tend not to go through major midcareer changes the way folks who work in other industries do. Rather than switch jobs, though, we tend to burn out instead.

LEAVING A POWERFUL LEGACY

While burnout in the health care field is a sad truth, we choose to focus on the uplifting side of it: People who work in health care are driven to make a difference, and the legacy they leave behind is the long list of people's lives they have touched. Have you ever seen the movie *Saving Private Ryan*, the World War II film starring Tom Hanks and Matt Damon? We're not going to ruin the plot for those of you who haven't seen it, but get out there and rent it; you'll thank us later. After watching it, spend some time reflecting on the scene at the end, where an older man asks his wife if he was a good man and if he had lived a good life. This scene is a sure tearjerker, but more than that, it's precisely the kind of thing we're talking about. When you look back at the life you have led, at home and at work, how do you want to feel?

When we think about our legacy as leaders, we want to look back and say, "Yes, I did as much as I could to touch the lives of those who worked with me." Don't you want to say this, too? Knowing you accomplished this goal means much more in life than simply balancing a budget or maximizing profits. Sure, these are important parts of what you do as a leader of your organization. Sure, driving higher employee engagement will also drive better financial performance. But in our opinion, focusing on the numbers shouldn't be the driving purpose behind why you do things.

Dr. David Feinberg, CEO of UCLA Health System, told us:

> We are in the business of taking care of people. It doesn't matter if you are a doctor, a nurse, or a janitor, or if you carry a leadership title, we all must champion and execute on the common goal of coming in every day to make sure we take care of our next patient.

That brings us back around to the point of this book: Building a culture of engagement within your organization is your way as a leader to leave an incredibly powerful legacy—one that will positively influence the lives of everyone you work with, now and into the future. Remember, we've written this book (and picked its provocative title) as a way to drive better experiences for our patients. After all, that's why we're all in the health care field in the first place.

MEASURING YOUR CULTURE IQ™

If you've come along with us this far, you'll know that we've covered lots of different topics in terms of how to build an organizational culture that drives employee engagement. But where does your organization stand on these issues? Have you just been reading along and nodding and saying, "Yup, we do that," and, "Yes, that sounds like my organization all right." Really? Are you sure? Let's be honest here and try to take an objective look at things. In fact, what would happen if you gave your associates a test of sorts that allows them to score how well the organization fosters employee engagement? Do you think they would give your organization the same score as you would?

To help you do just that, we've come up with the following self-assessment tool, which will determine your Culture IQ™ (or CIQ) score. Rather than just taking a guess at what level of employee engagement you think you have in your organization, you can use this easy and effective tool to find out where your organization actually ranks in terms of engagement.

Take five minutes to complete the following ten-question test, and encourage others in your organization to do the same. (You may notice something familiar about the ten questions: They loosely mirror the ten chapters you've just read.) Please rate each question on a scale of 1 to 10, with 1 being lowest and 10 being highest. In other words:

1 = We suck at this.
5 = We're headed in the right direction.
10 = We are rock stars!

Add up the total of your responses, and that's your CIQ score. Go ahead, take it!

1. Our core values are deeply ingrained into our decision-making process.
2. We have fun at work.
3. We have a system in place to show that we care about the personal lives of our employees.
4. We hire for fit in addition to skill.
5. We quickly and appropriately move the wrong people out of the organization.
6. Our employees get personally involved in our community service activities.
7. We regularly measure employee engagement, create action plans, and communicate results.
8. We have a robust reward and recognition program.
9. We execute on our commitment to growing and training our employees.
10. Our employees feel as though they are here for a purpose beyond just their job.

Now, in terms of evaluating your results after you've added up your score, we thought the following scale might be of use to you:

0–30:   Think about a career change.
31–50: Don't worry; there's hope.
51–75: You're on the right path—keep at it!
76–90: Consider yourselves special. Now keep it up!
91–100: Really? We'll take your word for it.

Look, if you're really interested in applying the power of CIQ in your organization, you're going to need to be honest when you take the test. So, if you gave yourself a score that landed somewhere between 0 and 30—try again. Were you being too harsh about your organization? Same goes if you scored above 90. If your organization is that great, how come we haven't heard of you? (Okay, maybe your organization really is that good. If so, get in touch!)

If you'd like to find out how your associates would score your organization, feel free to make copies of the sample test we have included in the appendix. Or you can take the test online at http://www.patientscomesecond.com, where we will also be posting the scores from other organizations so you can see how you and your team stack up. Who doesn't enjoy a little competition, right?

More important, using a tool like the CIQ score enables you and your associates to step outside the box . . . to think different and reconsider what everyone thinks they're supposed to do . . . to go for the chance of truly understanding the people you work with and what drives them. Then you can put yourself in line for the ultimate payday: delivering meaningful care to those who need it, an accomplishment that will far outstrip the value of your paycheck. Even so, don't build the kind of culture we describe in this book just for others; do it for yourself. You—and your patients—will be so happy you did.

Yes, things are changing all around us. But what if you began to see these changes as opportunities instead of threats? As Elliot Joseph, CEO of Hartford Healthcare, told us:

> This is clearly the most exciting time in my career, and I know at the same time a lot of my colleagues think it's the most uncertain time in our careers. I choose to see this as a historic moment of great opportunity and great excitement.

We understand that you might be nervous to undertake this journey. But you won't have to go it alone. Our goal in writing this book also includes building a community that will help stimulate and advance the conversation when it comes to the topic of employee engagement in health care organizations. Visit our website anytime for more information and leads on other leaders near you whom you can befriend, or reach out to us by picking up the phone or writing an e-mail. We would love to hear from you, and we promise to respond immediately!

We're all in this together, folks, and we look forward to sharing the ride with you. Let's enjoy the journey and make it an adventure. It's going to be fun.

GET YOUR CIQ SCORE

To get your Culture IQ™ (or CIQ) score, please rate your organization on a scale of 1 to 10 on the following statements:

1. Our core values are deeply ingrained into our decision-making process.
2. We have fun at work.
3. We have a system in place to show that we care about the personal lives of our employees.
4. We hire for fit in addition to skill.
5. We quickly and appropriately move the wrong people out of the organization.
6. Our employees get personally involved in our community service activities.
7. We regularly measure employee engagement, create action plans, and communicate results.
8. We have a robust reward and recognition program.
9. We execute on our commitment to growing and training our employees.
10. Our employees feel as though they are here for a purpose beyond just their job.

0–30:	Think about a career change.
31–50:	Don't worry; there's hope.
51–75:	You're on the right path—keep at it!
76–90:	Consider yourselves special. Now keep it up!
91–100:	Really? We'll take your word for it.

ACKNOWLEDGMENTS

We have lots of people to thank for their support of our journey. First of all, we want to say how much fun it has been to work together—lots of Saturday morning work sessions and conference calls, but all in the spirit of evangelizing our message. We'd like to give special thanks to Darren Dahl for helping put our long, incoherent diatribes into words that make sense. We are also ever grateful to our wives and kids for allowing us to do this (though we tried to work on it while you were asleep). And last but not least to our loyal, dedicated employees who have shown us time and again that if we care about them, they'll care about our patients.

Britt Berrett

Britt Berrett is the president of Texas Health Presbyterian Hospital Dallas, a 900-bed tertiary referral center that is part of the Texas Health Resources (THR) network. Prior to joining THR in 2010, Britt served as the president and chief executive officer of Medical City and Medical City Children's Hospital, the flagship medical center for the North Texas Division of HCA. He also served as a CEO as part of the SHARP Healthcare system in San Diego, California.

With over twenty years of both nonprofit and for-profit executive health care experience, Britt has navigated some of the most complicated organizational and environmental challenges in health care. But his health care journey began as a teenager while recovering in the Harborview Hospital Burn Unit in Seattle, Washington. It is there that he describes an overwhelming, almost spiritual connection with a team of dedicated and caring health care professionals who orchestrated a lifesaving effort for which he is profoundly grateful.

His journey in health care was later punctuated during a missionary experience in Peru in the 1980s, where he realized that excellence in a patient's experience was dependent upon a team of dedicated and well-coordinated caregivers. He completed his missionary experience, pursued a finance degree from Brigham Young University, and later completed a master's degree in health care from the Washington University School of Medicine in St. Louis, Missouri. He would later earn a PhD from the University of Texas at Dallas School of Economic, Political and Policy Sciences. His research focused on leadership theory in strategic planning.

In his executive role, his organizations have achieved recognition for exceptional organizational performance. Medical City was the first in North Texas to receive designation as a certified Magnet hospital by the American Nursing Credentialing Center, and Texas Health Resources was awarded the Best Place to Work by the *Dallas Business Journal*. Britt has experienced an inspiring level of success through his commitment to teams and organizational culture.

It was during these adventures that he connected with co-author Paul Spiegelman, and together they have spoken nationally and internationally on team dynamics and organizational culture. Britt is a dynamic and engaging presenter who speaks with personal experience and a driving passion for organizational excellence, whether it is to a local group of Boy Scout leaders or health care executives in Jeddah, Saudi Arabia. He is a guest lecturer at numerous colleges and organizations including BYU, SMU, UTD, UTA, ACHE, HFMA, AHA, and a whole number of other acronyms.

Britt has been accompanied on this journey by his wife, Lori, and children, Kelsey, Brad, and Gracie.

Paul Spiegelman

Paul Spiegelman is founder and CEO of The Beryl Companies, which includes: BerylHealth, a technology-focused patient experience company dedicated to improving relationships between health care providers and consumers; The Beryl Institute, a membership organization that serves the global community of practice as the premier thought leader on improving the patient experience in health care; The Circle, a training company that helps businesses enhance employee engagement and develop more positive workplace cultures; and The Small Giants Community, a global organization that brings together leaders who are focused on values-based business principles.

Paul started his health care business with his two brothers in 1985, bootstrapping a 24-7 operation in an eight-by-ten room with a cot. From the beginning, his passion was to help improve the patient experience. This came from his college experience of volunteering in the pediatric cancer ward at UCLA.

In building his company, he realized that the key to serving his customers was building an engaged, loyal workforce and has dedicated his career to improving the lives of his employees.

Paul is currently leading a unique, people-centric culture that has served over 750 health care organizations and has remarkably high employee and customer retention rates. BerylHealth has won nine "best place to work" awards, and in 2010, Paul was honored with the Ernst & Young Entrepreneur of the Year award.

Paul practiced law for two years prior to founding Beryl-Health. He holds a bachelor's degree in history from UCLA and a law degree from Southwestern University.

Paul is a sought-after speaker and author on executive leadership, entrepreneurship, corporate culture, customer relationships, and employee engagement. His views have been published in *Entrepreneur, The Dallas Morning News, Inc. Magazine, Healthcare Financial Management, Leadership Excellence,* and many other noteworthy publications, as well as in his first internationally published book, *Why Is Everyone Smiling?: The Secret Behind Passion, Productivity, and Profit.*

Paul connected with his coauthor Britt Berrett almost a decade ago, and they found an immediate connection around the topics of culture and engagement. After years of sharing stories and best practices, they hit the road to share their thoughts with other organizations, both inside and outside of health care. He has thoroughly enjoyed the collaboration with Britt on this book, and while Britt may be more outgoing, a comparison of their company videos shows that Paul has better dance moves.

To learn more about Paul, visit paulspiegelman.com.